*To Ali, Alison and Zoë, without whom there'd be no book*

## Publisher's Note

History is a serious business, but that's no reason for it not to be fun. *History Atlas* takes you on a light-hearted tour of the world, showing how humanity has changed and developed over thousands of years.

Clearly, that amounts to a lot of history, and we've had to make difficult choices about what to include. We're very sorry if we've missed out some of your favourite characters, but hope you'll meet many new favourites in the pages of this book. There are fifteen extraordinary worlds to explore, ranging from ancient Mesopotamia to our modern global world.

After reading all that, you'll be an expert historian – but we hope this will just be the start, and that this book will inspire you to discover more about the amazing (and sometimes awful) history of humanity. In the meantime, here's how to find your way around:

**1.** *The **introduction** to each chapter tells you a bit about that civilisation, and where and when it was at its height.*

**2.** *A 'map' of each civilisation introduces you to some of the key characters from that world. You'll find rulers, geniuses, villains, explorers, dancers and the occasional elephant. And a wombat. Every book should have a wombat.*

**3.** *On the **story** pages you'll find lots more fascinating facts and stories, including everything from how to write in hieroglyphs to the invention of the ice lolly.*

First published in the UK in 2020 by Alison Green Books
An imprint of Scholastic Children's Books
Euston House, 24 Eversholt Street, London NW1 1DB
A division of Scholastic Ltd
www.scholastic.co.uk
London – New York – Toronto – Sydney – Auckland – Mexico City – New Delhi – Hong Kong
Text and illustrations copyright © 2020 Thiago de Moraes
HB ISBN: 978 1 407189 23 9
All rights reserved. Moral rights asserted.
Cover designed by Zoë Tucker • Interior designed by Ali Halliday
With thanks to Rachel Phillipson for all the fact-checking.
The publisher has made every effort to ensure that
all facts are correct at the time of publication.
Printed in China
9 8 7 6 5 4 3 2 1
Papers used by Scholastic Children's Books are made from wood grown in sustainable forests.

FSC MIX Paper from responsible sources FSC® C008047 www.fsc.org

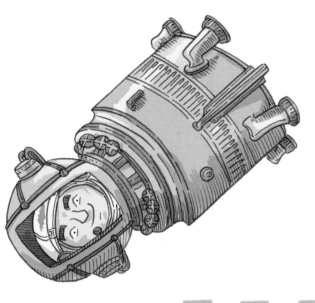

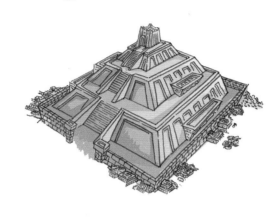

# Thiago de Moraes

# HISTORY ATLAS

*Heroes, villains and magnificent maps
from fifteen extraordinary civilisations*

ALISON GREEN BOOKS

*A navigation guide to the many remarkable,
ingenious and occasionally dastardly*

# WORLDS OF HISTORY

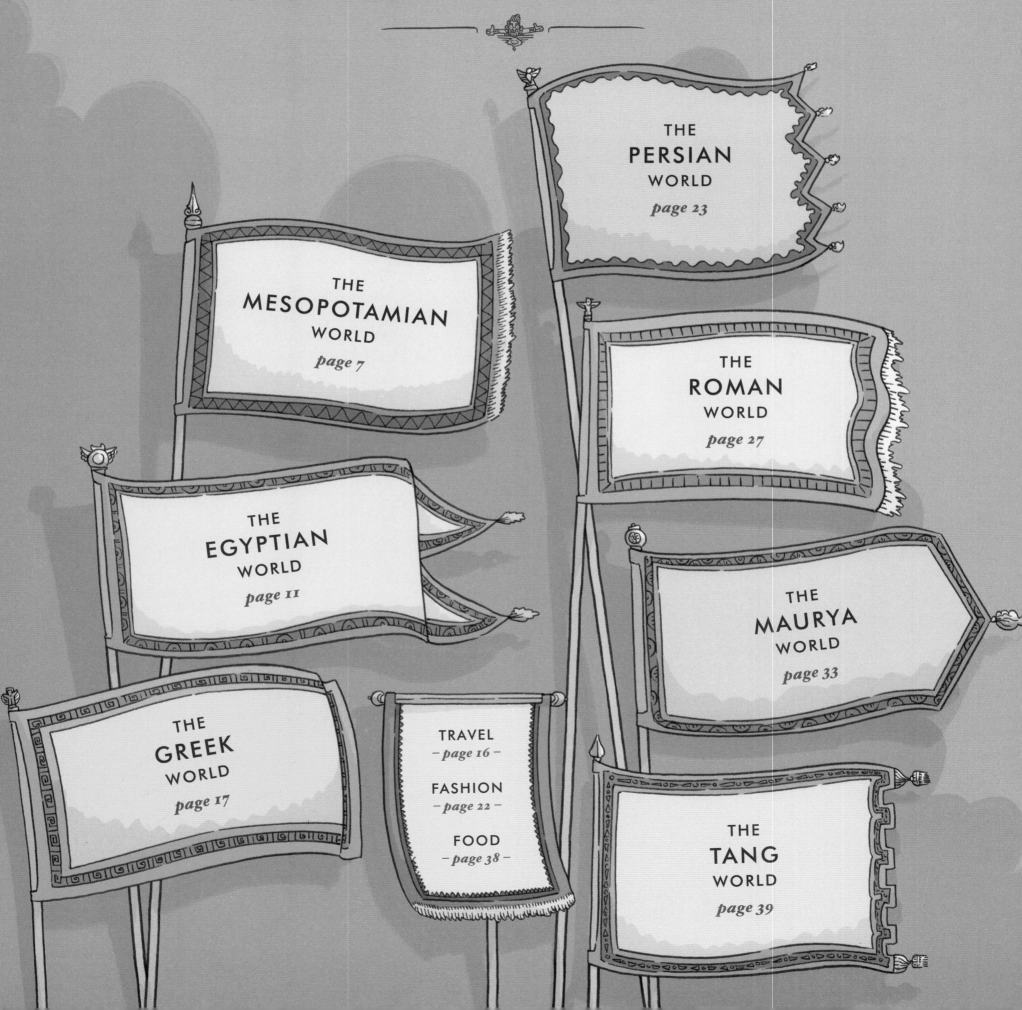

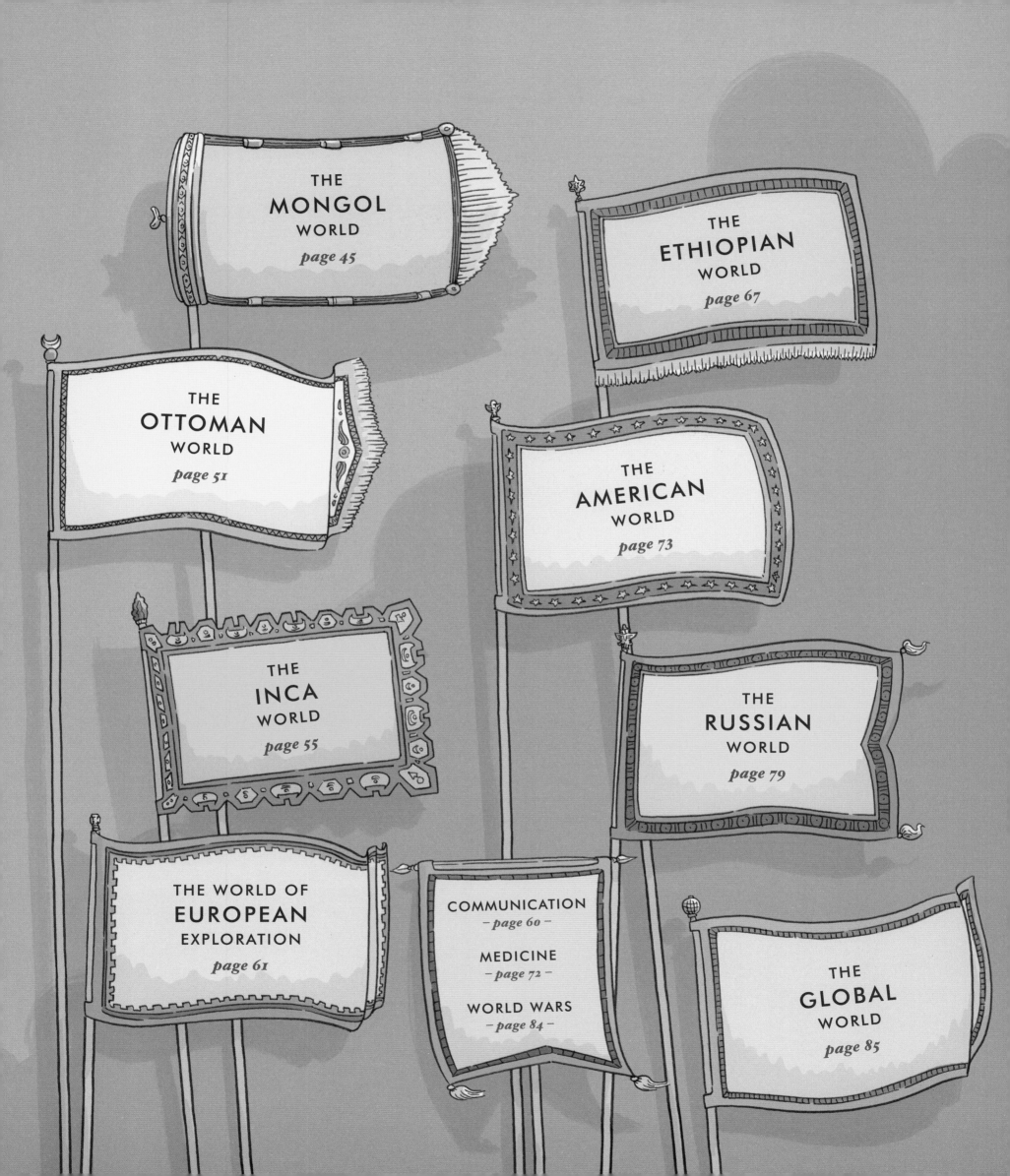

*Long before humans drew on the walls of caves, or wrote the first word, we've been telling stories about ourselves.*

You'll find all sorts of stories in this book: stories about humanity, and some of the things we've done over the past few thousand years. Not *all* of the things we've done: that would be a much, much bigger book, and you would have a hard time picking it up.

Our species, *homo sapiens* (it sort of means 'wise man' in Latin) has been around for over 300,000 years. For most of that time our ancestors got by without any of the things we have today. No reading or writing, no farming, no cities, no vehicles and, most importantly, no cake. People just roamed about, hunting animals, catching fish, foraging for fruit and nuts, and living wherever they could find shelter.

So how come we're not all still living like that? If there are two features that define our species, they're creativity and curiosity. (I bet you've already sneaked a peek at the rest of this book.) Humans love to investigate and improve. We're also quite good at inventing stuff – especially if it makes life easier.

It all started in the Stone Age. Over thousands of years humans made tools out of stone, bone and bits of antler. We got really good at it – but then, about 12,000 years ago, we made an even bigger discovery: if we planted crops and bred animals, we could feed a lot more people without having to keep moving all over the place.

The invention of farming changed everything. Now we could stay in one place all year round, and that made it worthwhile building houses. With some people growing all the food, other people had time to invent ingenious gadgets like wheels and boats. We could create art, music and all sorts of other things that make life more fun and interesting. We also had lots more time to wage war (we may have been clever, but we weren't necessarily sensible.)

Villages grew up. Then towns, and even cities. Civilisations developed everywhere: in deserts, jungles, mountains and across oceans. We tend to think that peoples and cultures from different parts of the world didn't meet each other until very recently, but that's not true at all. Whether on foot, horse or camel, in carriages or ships, humans have been travelling the globe and mingling with one another since the beginning of history.

From the moment human life started in Africa, we've been on the move. From Africa, we made our way all round the globe. During the Bronze Age, people were already trading goods all over Europe, Asia and Africa. Over two thousand years ago, traders were travelling the Silk Road from China to Europe. As people moved about, they exchanged ideas, inventions, language and culture. They also fought each other a heck of a lot.

This book is an attempt to tell the stories of some of these peoples – how they began, what they achieved and how they helped create the world we live in today. It's also an excuse for me to draw lots of little people with swords.

Now you're ready to start travelling through history. Remember to have fun and don't trust anything you read too much: there are countless ways of telling a story (or a history) and this is only one.

*Thiago de Moraes*

**Thiago de Moraes**

# The Mesopotamian World

## *How to make a city — with laws, wheels and swanky gardens*

If you want to set up a city, it's a good idea to find a river — or two rivers, in this case: the mighty Tigris and Euphrates. (Mesopotamia means 'land between the rivers' in Greek.) Rivers provide water for drinking and for watering crops, so it's no surprise that some of the world's very first cities were built here.

Over some three thousand years, humans in Mesopotamia gradually worked out how to live in really big groups. It wasn't easy. When lots of people live together there are bound to be arguments, and that meant inventing laws. They also needed to keep count of all the things they farmed, made and traded, so they came up with the world's first system of writing. That's right, writing was invented by accountants.

Some of the earliest people in Mesopotamia were the Sumerians. They were an inventive lot, who worked out how to make sailing boats, wheels, and maps. They were also seriously good at maths and astronomy.

They soon had competition, though, as the Akkadians, Assyrians and Babylonians set up rival city states. The Babylonians were particularly fearsome fighters. Surprisingly, they were also amazing gardeners, and their capital city, Babylon, was renowned for its beautiful gardens.

From around 3500 to 600 BC

### THE MAP OF THE MESOPOTAMIAN WORLD

Several magnificent city states grew up in this area (now home to parts of many countries including Iraq, Syria and Turkey.) The Sumerians started it, creating towns like Ur and Eridu. The others copied them — then spent most of their time fighting and trying to outdo each other.

NINEVEH
ASHUR
RIVER EUPHRATES
RIVER TIGRIS
AKKAD
BABYLON
SUSA
URUK
ERIDU   UR

LANGUAGE
Sumerian, Akkadian
(and many others)

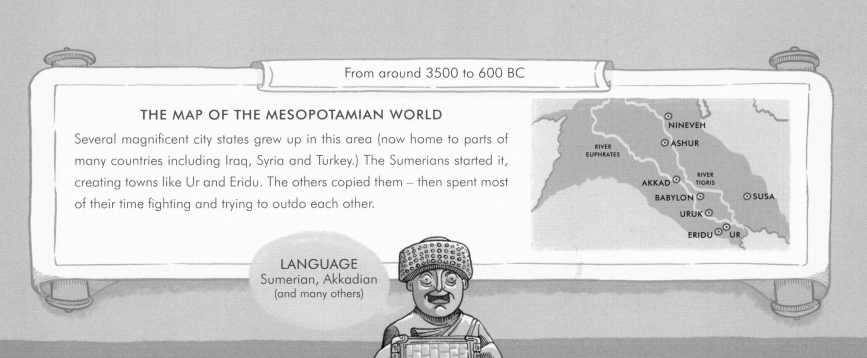

A representation of

# the Mesopotamian world

including hanging gardens, lumpy beer, winged lions and a very heavy library.

**6 FARMING**
Mesopotamians pretty much invented farming, and most people worked on the land. Thanks to them, people in the cities had plenty to eat and could get on with other jobs – like inventing wheels, weapons, sailboats and beer.

**7 OX-DRAWN PLOUGHS**
The Sumerians had the bright idea of getting animals to pull their ploughs. Life was much easier after that – though probably not for the animals.

**8 KUBABA**
Kubaba is famous for being the first recorded female ruler in history. After an early life as a tavern keeper, she became queen of Kish – quite an impressive career move.

**9 UR-NAMMU**
A king of Ur. He's best known for establishing the oldest set of laws ever found, which he modestly called The Code of Ur-Nammu. Most punishments involved paying him a fine in silver, or execution.

**10 HAMMURABI**
A great Babylonian king. He created a set of laws, the Code of Hammurabi, to make sure everyone was treated fairly. Unfortunately, his laws said you had to prove your innocence by being thrown in a river. If you drowned, you were guilty.

**11 LAMASSU**
The Assyrians built these huge statues of bulls and lions to protect their palaces and temples. They had human heads, the wings of an eagle, and represented the stars and constellations in the night sky.

**12 GILGAMESH**
One of the first kings of Uruk. He's also the main character in the *Epic of Gilgamesh*. We don't know much about him, but the *Epic* says he was the son of a god, built the city walls by himself and ruled for 126 years. A likely story.

**13 KISH**
Where you have rivers, you generally have mud. That's why great walled cities such as Kish were mainly built with mud bricks.

**1 BABYLON**
The grand capital of the Babylonian empire. The city became famous for its hanging gardens. We haven't a clue what they looked like – but we do know that most people back then thought it was bonkers to plant pretty things that you couldn't eat.

**2 ASHUR**
A super-grand city built by the Assyrians. It had over thirty temples, several palaces, and a library of clay tablets, which they'd nicked from Babylon.

**3 SARGON THE GREAT**
The son of a gardener who became a mighty warrior king. Sargon led the Akkadians and conquered most of the Mesopotamian states. He also had a really big beard.

**4 STELES**
Huge stone slabs where important things were written for everyone to see. A lot of what we know about Mesopotamia comes from steles.

**5 ENMEBARAGESI**
Most information about Sumerian rulers comes from 'The List of Kings' – a long list written on a stone tablet. It's not the most reliable source: it tells us some kings ruled for thousands of years, and other porkies. The first king we can prove existed for sure is Enmebaragesi of Kish.

## 17 BEER
The Mesopotamians didn't invent beer, but they drank a lot of it. Their beer looked like porridge, and they used straws to stop them swallowing all sorts of yucky bits and little stones that were left in the drink.

## 18 SHULGI
Son of Ur-Nammu. While his dad impressed everyone by writing laws, Shulgi tried something a bit different: he ran 100 miles between two cities in a single day to show people how strong he was.

## 19 SAIL BOATS
The first sail boats were just bits of wood topped with a fabric sail. They couldn't be steered, so pretty much drifted with the wind. Luckily, better boat designs were soon invented, which was handy if you actually wanted to get somewhere.

## 20 ENHEDUANNA
Writing things down was a very new concept in ancient times. Sargon's daughter, Enheduanna, is the very first writer in the world whose name we know. She wrote beautiful poetry and prayers, and was a powerful high priestess.

## 14 SENNACHERIB
Ruler of the Assyrian empire. He was fascinated by engineering and farming, and wasn't shy when it came to displaying his power. When the Babylonians refused to accept his rule he destroyed their city.

## 15 UR
One of the biggest cities in the ancient world, with over 65,000 inhabitants. The huge temple in the middle is called a ziggurat. It was dedicated to the moon god, Nanna, and even had a kitchen where priests could prepare food for him.

## 16 NARAM-SIN
Sargon's grandson. He expanded the Akkadian empire and battled almost every single one of his neighbours. He became quite big-headed, and told everyone to treat him as a god.

## 21 ASHURBANIPAL
This Assyrian king was a ruthless warrior who claimed he could strangle a lion with his bare hands. But he was equally proud of being a scholar, and created the world's first library, collecting over 20,000 clay tablets.

## 22 NEBUCHADNEZZAR II
The king who rebuilt Babylon after it had been destroyed by Sennacherib. He created amazing buildings, and hanging gardens that were one of the seven wonders of the ancient world. He was even a good ruler, giving women equal rights with men.

# Mesopotamian Life

A lot of good ideas, such as inventing the wheel or writing things down, seem to have occurred to many people all over the world at around the same time – about 5,000 years ago. However, most of the earliest examples come from Mesopotamia.

## LAYING DOWN THE LAW

One of the world's oldest sets of laws, the Code of Hammurabi, comes from Mesopotamia. It contains a lot of stuff about cutting people's fingers off, or even executing them for breaking the law, but it also introduced some really sound ideas, like a minimum wage for workers.

## MUDDY THINKING

The Sumerians came up with one of the earliest forms of writing, called cuneiform. It involved scratching marks on clay tablets, and was used for over 3,000 years. Writing meant people could keep records and send each other letters (which they put in mud envelopes – postmen must have been seriously strong in those days.) The Sumerians were also the first people to write down a story: *The Epic of Gilgamesh*, about the many adventures of super-strong King Gilgamesh of Uruk.

## ROUND THINGS WITH A HOLE

Mesopotamians developed two handy round things with a hole in the middle: the wheel, and the number 0. The first wheels were actually potters' wheels. It was ages before people thought, 'Hey, we could roll that wheel over the ground and use it to carry stuff!'

The Babylonians, meanwhile, were incredibly whizzy at maths. Their best invention was the number 0. That might seem like nothing, but try doing sums without it. Not easy.

# The Egyptian World

## *Bossy kings, bolshy peasants and crazy tombs*

Ancient Egyptian society was built on very strict rules, and everyone was expected to know their place. At the top of the tree were Egypt's kings, called pharaohs. They represented the power of the gods on earth and were incredibly bossy.

Most people, of course, were peasants, and they had pretty horrible lives. But ancient Egypt is full of surprises. For instance, when the pharaoh didn't pay his peasants' wages, they went on the world's first-ever strike – and won. Egypt's women also had almost equal rights with men, which shocked the ancient Greeks when they invaded.

The Egyptians had many skills, from writing and glass-making to boat-building and some quite effective medicine. They were even the first to bake bread. Their love of order also meant they were great at constructing enormous, complicated buildings, like the extraordinary pyramids which they built as tombs for their pharaohs. To this day we're not quite sure how they managed it.

Ancient Egyptian society remained surprisingly unchanged for all of its 3,000 years – until they were conquered not once, but three times. First came the Persians; then Alexander the Great, and finally the Romans. With the death of Cleopatra (who you'll find in the Roman World), the reign of the pharaohs finally came to an end.

From 3000 to 30 BC

### THE MAP OF THE EGYPTIAN WORLD

Ancient Egypt was in northeast Africa, where modern-day Egypt (and a bit of Sudan) still stands. As in Mesopotamia, life revolved around a great river: the Nile. Its annual flooding made the land incredibly fertile, and Egypt's main towns were dotted along its banks.

LANGUAGE
Egyptian

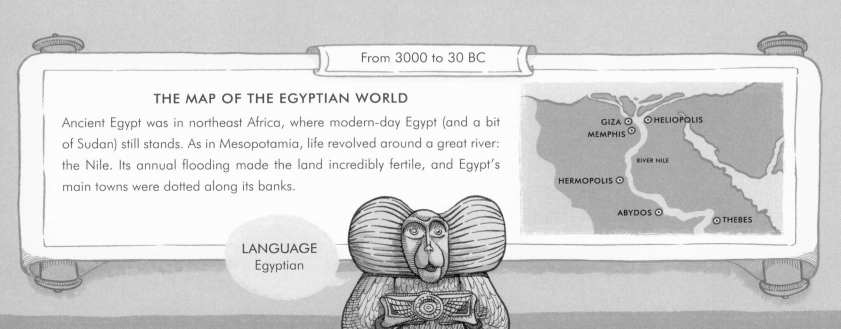

GIZA
HELIOPOLIS
MEMPHIS
RIVER NILE
HERMOPOLIS
ABYDOS
THEBES

## A depiction of the cities, tombs and temples of *the Egyptian world*

featuring huge pyramids, god-like pharaohs, hungry crocodiles and a really big river.

**1 KHUFU**
A pharaoh who wanted to make really, really sure people would remember him after he died. He had the Great Pyramid at Giza built to use as his tomb.

**2 HEMIUNU**
The architect who designed Khufu's Great Pyramid. He did a great job on the outside. The inside's a bit boring, though – just some small, plain burial chambers and a few corridors.

**3 PYRAMIDS**
When pharaohs died, their bodies were turned into mummies and placed in these huge tombs, together with all they needed for the afterlife: treasure, ships, and even pets and servants. Over a hundred still stand in Egypt today.

**4 MEMPHIS**
Egypt's capital for many years. Thousands of workers were kept busy here, building temples and tombs for the pharaohs. It's said the city's white-painted walls gleamed in the sun.

**5 PRIESTS**
As well as looking after their gods in temples, Egyptian priests were thought to have magical powers – looking into the future, healing people, and sometimes cursing them, too.

**6 SOBEKNEFERU**
Most rulers in ancient times were men. Egypt was unusual in having a few female pharaohs, and Sobekneferu is the first one we know of.

**7 RAMSES THE GREAT**
Ramses ordered many of Egypt's greatest tombs and temples to be built. He also lived to be over 90 years old. In an era when most people died at 30, that feels like a bigger achievement.

**8 DOCTORS**
As well as using magic to try and cure people, Egyptians also had pretty good doctors (by the standards of the time). They developed medicines, set bones and even performed surgery (but without anaesthetic – ouch!)

**9 VALLEY OF THE KINGS**
Some of Egypt's best-known rulers were buried here, including Ramses the Great and Tutankhamun. Their tombs were cut directly into the rock in an attempt to foil grave-robbers.

**10 AHMES**
A scribe who wrote a papyrus full of very clever mathematical puzzles. It was written in 1550 BC. See if you can work out how long ago that was.

**11 AKHENATEN**
A revolutionary pharaoh who forced Egyptians to worship his brand-new sun-god, Aten, instead of the 1,000 or so fun gods they had before. Most Egyptians thought he was mad, and changed everything back after he died.

**12 TUTANKHAMUN**
Akhenaten's son. He became pharaoh as a child and died at 19. He still found time to undo a lot of his dad's revolutionary changes, and bring back all the old gods that Egyptians liked.

**13 NEFERTITI**
Akhenaten's favourite wife. She ruled the country with him and was famous for her looks – her name means 'the beautiful one has come'.

**14 SCRIBES**
Scribes were the only non-noble people who knew how to write. It took years to train, and they were highly valued. Scribes recorded everything, from laws and medical procedures to food stocks and magic spells.

**15 THEBES**
Another capital, and a very important centre of Egyptian religion. Thebes was famous for an area called Karnak, a huge, spectacular complex of temples, obelisks and sphinxes.

**16 HATSHEPSUT**
The longest-ruling woman in Egyptian history. She was an excellent pharaoh but had to put up with having statues made of her wearing a little fake beard (something all pharaoh statues had to have).

**17 FARMERS**
Most Egyptians worked as farmers, but only for two-thirds of the year. When the Nile flooded, they had a good rest. Just joking: that's when they were forced to build stuff for the pharaohs.

**18 AMENHOTEP**
An architect who designed and built a number of great temples. The pharaoh was so impressed, he proclaimed the architect a god, and gave him his own temple (which Amenhotep probably had to build himself).

**19 MENES**
Egypt used to be two countries. Lower Egypt's king wore a flat, red crown; Upper Egypt's wore a white, conical one. Menes unified the two Egypts – which meant he could wear a groovy new united red-and-white crown.

**20 HELIOPOLIS**
Egyptians believed this city was built on the site where the world was created by the god Atum. Heliopolis means 'city of the sun' in Greek, and one of Egypt's most popular gods, the sun-god Ra, was worshipped here.

**21 ARMIES**
The Egyptian army started out as a temporary force of untrained farmers and peasants. The pharaohs eventually created an army of professional soldiers – probably much to the relief of the farmers and peasants.

**22 THUTMOSE III**
One of Egypt's greatest pharaohs, Thutmose was a just ruler and a brilliant warrior. He conquered many other lands and was much loved by the Egyptians (but not so much by their neighbours.)

**23 REKHMIRE**
Vizier to Thutmose III. Viziers were powerful, as they pretty much ran the country for the pharaoh. Luckily, an inscription on Rekhmire's tomb says he prided himself on being merciful to the poor.

# Writing Hieroglyphs

## PLEASE DRAW YOUR SIGNATURE HERE, SIR

Egyptian hieroglyphs are one of the world's oldest forms of writing. Instead of using an alphabet, they drew small pictures to represent different sounds, objects and ideas.

Hieroglyphs were pretty tricky to read and memorise – there were over 700 symbols, representing everything from a pyramid to a rabbit. Compare that with just 26 'symbols'

in our English alphabet (which we inherited from the Romans). Here are some of the most common sound hieroglyphs, and how some famous names were written:

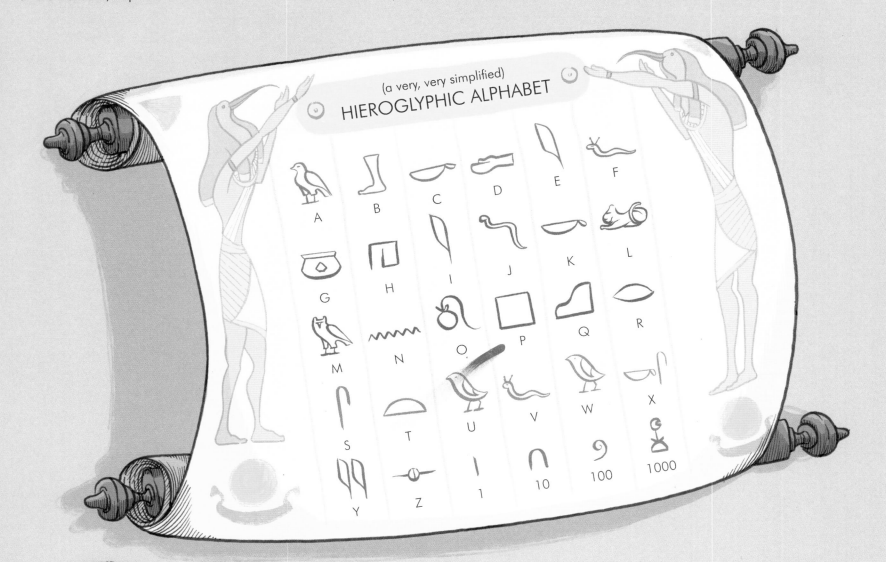

(a very, very simplified)
HIEROGLYPHIC ALPHABET

A B C D E F
G H I J K L
M N O P Q R
S T U V W X
Y Z 1 10 100 1000

This is how some pharaohs' names were written. The oval line around the hieroglyphs is called a cartouche. It means the name belongs to a member of the royal family. The names here are written in short versions – the pharaohs' full names are much, much longer when written (it must've taken ages to sign stuff).

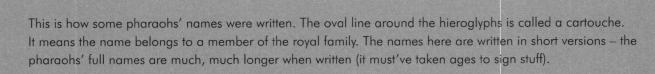

Khufu    Hatshepsut    Thutmose III    Akhenaten    Tutankhamun    Ramses II

# Building Khufu's Great Pyramid

## BETWEEN A ROCK AND, WELL, ANOTHER ROCK

Pharaohs spent a lot of time worrying about how to look important in the afterlife. The key thing was to have a massive tomb or monument – and what could be more impressive than a pyramid?

The huge pyramids at Giza, near Memphis, show just what amazing engineers the ancient Egyptians were. The largest was built for Khufu. It's over 140m high and for over 3,000 years it was the tallest structure in the world.

Pyramids were made from huge blocks of stone, each of which weighed upwards of two tonnes. It took some 2.3 million blocks to build Khufu's pyramid, and no one is sure how the Egyptians did it. One theory is that they made ramps around the buildings and pulled the blocks up using ropes.

Pyramids were built with incredible precision, and architects went to great lengths to conceal the entrance. Pharaohs were buried with loads of treasure, which was a great temptation for robbers. Despite their best efforts, most pyramids were looted soon after the pharaoh died. Sometimes even the mummified pharaoh was stolen.

Eventually, pharaohs decided pyramids just weren't safe enough. Instead they created a new burial ground in the desert, with secret tombs carved directly into the rocks. The robbers still found most of them, though.

*Originally pyramids were covered in fine white limestone – not easy to keep clean in a dusty desert.*

*Here's the pharaoh inspecting the building works.*

*A huge sphinx guarded the pyramids – a mythical creature with a human head and the body of a lion.*

# ON THE MOVE
## *Travelling through the ages*

Humans don't like staying put – in fact we've been moving around for thousands of years.
Here are a few ways of getting about, with an estimate of how far the very fastest and fittest of them
could take you, non-stop, in a day (well, in 16 hours – everybody needs their sleep.)

### THE FOOT *80km per day*
The original (and still very popular) way of getting around. Humans have walked pretty
much the entire globe on foot. Sure, it takes ages, but you get to see the sights.

### THE HORSE *100km per day*
People started domesticating horses around 3500 BC, but it took a lot longer to invent things like
stirrups and saddles, which made riding easier and more comfortable (for the rider, not the horse).
Horses can gallop much faster than this, but they can't keep it up all day.

### THE BOAT *800km per day (e.g. a Polynesian sailing canoe)*
People started making boats some 10,000 years ago. They hollowed out tree trunks and used
oars to propel them. The invention of the sail, two thousand years later, really moved things
along. The Polynesians, for example, sailed all over the Pacific Ocean in small sailing canoes.

### THE STEAM ENGINE *3,200km per day (e.g. the 4468 Mallard)*
Steam power had been around for ages, but the first steam-powered
trains were invented in the early 1800s AD. The Mallard was the
fastest steam locomotive of all time. It was no lame duck.

### THE CAR
*1,800km per day (e.g. a regular car on a motorway)*
Slower than trains, but much more handy, the first cars
were invented in the late 1800s AD.

The fastest cars today can go at 400km per
hour, but you'd get arrested if you tried that on a
motorway. Sadly, 15km per hour is more like it in
our congested cities.

### THE AEROPLANE
*13,000km per day (e.g. the Boeing 747)*
The first aeroplanes were basically big gliders that
flew for a bit, then crashed. It took courage and
cleverness to create today's huge passenger planes.

One special plane, Concorde,
was over twice as fast as your
average plane, but was so
expensive to maintain that it's
not in use anymore.

### THE SPACE ROCKET *640,000km per day (e.g. Apollo 10)*
It takes serious speed to leave Earth's gravity and fly to the moon, so it's no surprise
that the fastest manned craft ever invented was a rocket ship. Rockets can't really
keep this speed up for a whole day, but it's more fun to pretend they can.

# The Greek World
## *Thinker, sailor, soldier, gym bunny*

The ancient Greeks liked to keep busy – and very, very fit. They were a restless, inquisitive, competitive lot, who thought that having perfectly toned tummy muscles was every bit as important as being brainy.

They were obsessed with personal glory, and turned anything and everything into a competition: art, philosophy, sport, you name it. It sounds really tiring, but it led to some outstanding achievements. In fact, it's fair to say we all owe a lot to the Greeks. Among other things, they came up with democracy, western-style theatre, the Olympic Games – and working out at the gym.

It wasn't all fun and games, though. Unlike the huge kingdoms of Egypt and Persia, ancient Greece was mostly a bunch of independent city states. They had a lot in common, but that didn't mean they liked each other much. They fought one another tooth and nail – and picked fights with their neighbours, too. Unsurprisingly, these madly ambitious keep-fit fanatics were rather good at fighting, and the Greeks gradually took over a huge area of land.

All this conquering didn't make them very popular, though, and eventually Philip II from next-door Macedon conquered them right back. Philip's son, Alexander the Great, was even more successful. He stretched the empire all the way to India, and spread Greek culture halfway across the world.

From around 800 to 300 BC

### THE MAP OF THE GREEK WORLD

The first Greek states developed about 1000 BC, around the eastern Mediterranean and Aegean seas (where modern-day Greece and parts of Turkey are). Later, Alexander the Great extended the empire from Egypt to India.

BYZANTIUM

MACEDON

TROY

ATHENS

OLYMPIA

SYRACUSE   SPARTA

RHODES

CRETE

MEDITERRANEAN SEA

ALEXANDRIA

LANGUAGE
Greek
(various dialects)

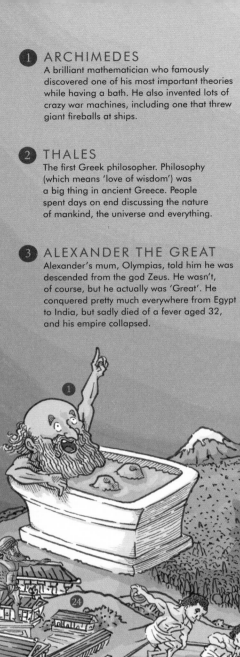
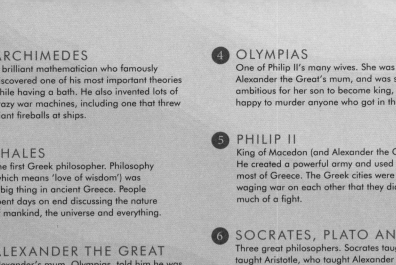
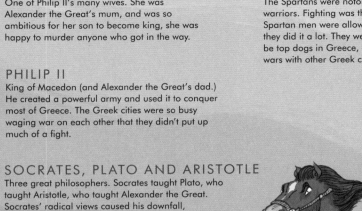

## 1 ARCHIMEDES
A brilliant mathematician who famously discovered one of his most important theories while having a bath. He also invented lots of crazy war machines, including one that threw giant fireballs at ships.

## 2 THALES
The first Greek philosopher. Philosophy (which means 'love of wisdom') was a big thing in ancient Greece. People spent days on end discussing the nature of mankind, the universe and everything.

## 3 ALEXANDER THE GREAT
Alexander's mum, Olympias, told him he was descended from the god Zeus. He wasn't, of course, but he actually was 'Great'. He conquered pretty much everywhere from Egypt to India, but sadly died of a fever aged 32, and his empire collapsed.

## 4 OLYMPIAS
One of Philip II's many wives. She was Alexander the Great's mum, and was so ambitious for her son to become king, she was happy to murder anyone who got in the way.

## 5 PHILIP II
King of Macedon (and Alexander the Great's dad.) He created a powerful army and used it to conquer most of Greece. The Greek cities were so busy waging war on each other that they didn't put up much of a fight.

## 6 SOCRATES, PLATO AND ARISTOTLE
Three great philosophers. Socrates taught Plato, who taught Aristotle, who taught Alexander the Great. Socrates' radical views caused his downfall, though, and he was sentenced to die by drinking poison. Luckily, he was very philosophical about it.

## 7 SPARTA
The Spartans were notoriously ruthless warriors. Fighting was the only job Spartan men were allowed to do, and they did it a lot. They were determined to be top dogs in Greece, and fought big wars with other Greek cities like Athens.

## 8 HIPPARCHIA
Hipparchia scandalised everyone by rejecting her rich background to become a Cynic philosopher. Cynics believed in living the simplest life possible, so she lived in the streets, dressed like a bloke, and shocked men with her outspoken views.

## 9 HERODOTUS
Considered the first historian, Herodotus wrote about the Greco-Persian wars and his travels around the world. He liked mixing in the odd fib, though, and told tall tales about flying dragons and one-eyed men stealing gold from griffins.

## 24 OLYMPIA
The Olympic Games took place here, around a huge temple of Zeus (lord of all the Greek gods). It was named after Mount Olympus, where Greeks believed their gods lived.

A depiction of
# the Greek world
including elegant temples, ruthless warriors, lots of marble and a big wooden horse.

## 22 LYCURGUS
Possibly a mythical character, he's credited as the creator of Sparta's super-tough laws. These compelled all boys over seven to go into brutal military training. Children were even kept hungry, so they'd learn how to steal food without getting caught.

## 23 SOPHOCLES, AESCHYLUS AND EURIPIDES
Three playwrights whose plays are still performed today. They hogged a lot of prizes at the annual Greek drama festival and are best known for writing spectacular tragedies full of death.

## 20 ARTEMISIA
Queen of the Greek city-state of Halicarnassus. Female warriors were rare back then, but Artemisia was brave, clever, commanded a fleet of ships, and helped out King Xerxes of Persia during his invasion of Greece.

## 21 PHILIPPIDES
An Athenian courier. It's said he ran 250km before the Battle of Marathon to ask Sparta for help against the Persians. After the battle he ran another 42km to tell the Athenians that the Greeks had won. That distance is still celebrated in today's marathon races.

## 10 ATHENS
One of the most powerful Greek city states. Athens was renowned for its brilliant artists, philosophers, playwrights and scientists. It was so impressive, even the Spartans didn't destroy it after they conquered it.

## 11 ASPASIA
A teacher, writer and philosopher who spent lots of time discussing clever stuff with people like Socrates and Plato. She was also Pericles' girlfriend, and it's claimed she wrote some of his greatest speeches.

## 12 PERICLES
Pericles was teased for having a very long head, so he always wore a helmet to disguise it. But his name means 'surrounded by glory', and Athens had a golden age under his leadership. Art, literature, philosophy and democracy flourished, and the city became an empire.

## 13 CLEISTHENES
An Athenian leader who is called 'The Father of Democracy'. He introduced a system in which all citizens (well, all male ones, anyway) could vote for laws and choose their own leaders.

## 14 SOLON
One of the 'Seven Wise Men of Greece'. Solon created a whole load of new laws for Athens, that reduced the power of the rich, and made life much fairer for the poor. He needed a break after all that, and spent the next ten years on holiday.

## 15 PHIDIAS
A master sculptor who created amazing statues of the gods. Greeks found his work so awe-inspiring, they said he must have actually met the gods themselves.

## 16 LEONIDAS
A Spartan king who led a small force of Greek soldiers into battle against the vast Persian army at Thermopylae. He and his men were all wiped out in the end, but they put up a heck of a fight. (Spartan warriors never, ever gave in.)

## 17 TROY
One of the ancient Greeks' most popular myths tells how their ancestors united to attack the city of Troy. Their cunning plan was to pretend to run away, while actually hiding inside a huge wooden horse. Not the most straightforward plan, but it worked.

## 19 SAPPHO
Most Greek poets were men, so Sappho was unusual in being a much-admired female poet. In fact, her poetry made her so famous, the ancient Greeks put her face on everything from vases to coins.

## 18 HOMER
The ancient Greeks' best-loved poet. His greatest poems are The Iliad, which is full of battles, heroes and tragedy, and The Odyssey, which features a six-headed monster, a one-eyed giant and creatures who lure sailors to their death with their beautiful singing.

# Greek Life
## JOLLY GOOD SPORTS

Greeks loved all sorts of contests, and the Olympic Games were the greatest of all. Every four years, all the peoples of Greece would gather together to honour their main god, Zeus, and compete against each other in lots of sports.

Even though the Greek states spent lots of time fighting, the games happened regularly for more than a thousand years. The winners would get an olive-leaf wreath and become very famous (until the next games, that is).

Our modern Olympic Games are modelled on the Greeks', and contain some of the same sports. Other ancient Olympic practices seem really weird to us, as does their tradition of competing completely naked (which is why we've put loin cloths on them here.)

### Wrestling and boxing
*Greeks loved boshing each other. There were very few rules in Greek wrestling. The only things contestants couldn't do were biting their opponent or poking them in the eye.*

### Taking oaths
*Before the games started all participants would pray and offer sacrifices for victory – or death. That's how seriously they took the whole thing.*

### Female sports
*Married women weren't allowed to watch the games, presumably because all the sportsmen were naked. Odd, then, that unmarried women were allowed to watch. They also had their own games, with running races, in honour of the goddess Hera.*

### Boys' Games
*Boys between 12 and 18 competed separately, racing, boxing and wrestling each other.*

## PLAYING AROUND

Greeks loved watching plays and built spectacular amphitheatres all over their world. The bowl shape gave the theatre amazing acoustics – actors could easily be heard even in the cheap seats at the back.

Early Greek theatre featured a simple performance by just one actor. Gradually, it became more and more complex, as they invented the use of scenery, a raised stage, and multiple actors.

Greeks were the first to divide drama into tragedy (a sad story with a lot of death) and comedy (a funny story, usually with a lot of rude jokes).

Several ancient Greek plays are still performed today – not bad after 3,000 years.

## Pentathlon

*Athletes performed five sports – wrestling, javelin, long jump, discus and running – in a single afternoon. In case that wasn't hard enough, they jumped holding weights to propel them further.*

## Winning

*The only official prize was an olive wreath. However, famous athletes could erect a statue of themselves in the temple of Zeus; some had songs and poems written about them and others were given free food for life in their cities (obviously the greatest prize of all).*

## Running

*Like today, there were all sorts of running races. In the toughest, athletes had to run wearing full armour.*

## Chariot Racing

*Horse-drawn chariots raced twelve laps round the track. This was by far the most dangerous sport, with massive crashes and lots of injuries and deaths.*

## VOTES FOR (ALMOST) ALL

For most of human history a few very powerful and rich people (kings, queens, pharaohs, tyrants, etc) have told a lot of very poor people what to do. Some Greek states tried to find fairer ways to live, and democracy was one of these ways. ('Democracy' means 'rule of the people'.)

In democratic Greek states, all citizens could vote to elect leaders and establish laws. That sounds great – but sadly not all *people* were *citizens*. Women, slaves and foreigners didn't get a vote, which wasn't fair at all.

## SEEING STARS

The Greeks were the first people to work out that the world wasn't flat like a pancake. They did this by observing that the stars in the sky looked different when seen from different parts of the world. They eventually calculated the earth's circumference by measuring the length of shadows in different places. Pretty clever stuff.

# THE HEIGHT OF FASHION

*How we learned to look cool (while keeping warm)*

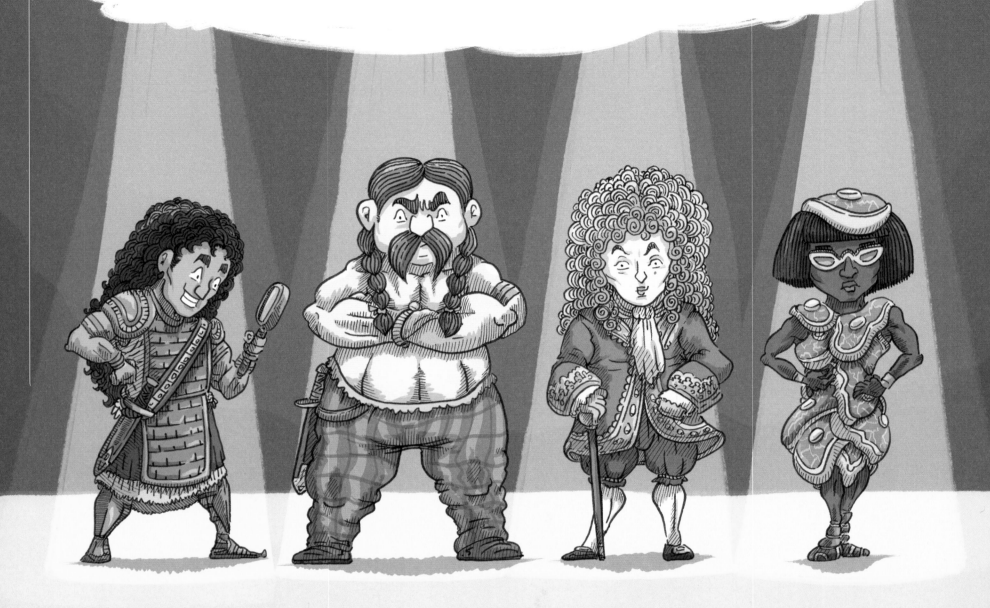

### MIRROR, MIRROR ON THE WALL (OF YOUR GRAVE)

We think of Bronze Age warriors as big brutes carrying axes. However, these fearsome fighters also cared a lot about their looks. Bronze Age graves contain a surprising number of beauty implements: tweezers, mirrors, combs and scissors, as well as weapons and jewels. You clearly want to look good if you're going to smash someone's face in.

### WHO WEARS THE TROUSERS?

Roman clothes were all a bit like dresses: tunics, togas and other loose-fitting garments. When Julius Caesar fought the tribes of Gaul and Germany, he wrote back home to say how shocking it was to see them wearing a totally barbaric, uncivilised item of clothing: trousers.

### WE'VE GOT IT COVERED

Fashionable men in the 17th and 18th centuries proudly sported huge powdered wigs called perukes. A lot of people at the time suffered from a horrible, incurable disease called syphilis, which made their hair fall out, so they wore wigs to hide their bald heads. So many men wore these wigs, they became the height of fashion, even for healthy people.

### WHERE FASHION MEATS ART

These days fashion designers create ever more extraordinary clothes that are very hard to wear and cost loads. Their many crazy creations include shoes that look like armadillos and a skirt with an actual carousel around it. The award for the most unusual must go to a dress made completely out of raw meat. A terrible waste of good steak.

# The Persian World

## *From roaming all over to ruling all over*

The Persians did astonishingly well for a bunch of nomadic warriors. They clobbered their neighbours (then their neighbours' neighbours; then their neighbours' neighbours' neighbours), creating the largest empire the world had ever seen.

Persian rulers became staggeringly rich and powerful – but they were also famously tolerant, as kings go. Unlike many conquerors, they didn't force their new subjects to change their language, religion or customs. They just asked people to live together peacefully (and to pay their taxes. There's always a catch, isn't there?)

The empire became so huge, it was like a bridge between East and West. Everyone who wanted to travel between Africa, Europe and the East had to pass through it, and it became an unbelievably diverse, creative melting pot of people and ideas.

It wasn't easy ruling all those different peoples using only hand-written letters, horses and boats. Luckily, the Persians were nifty organisers. They built great roads between their cities, and set up an impressively speedy postal service. Like the Mesopotamians before them, they even found time to do a spot of gardening.

Then who should spoil it all but Alexander the Great. He swooped down from Greece and took over the empire. When he died, his generals divided the Persian provinces between themselves – and promptly started fighting each other.

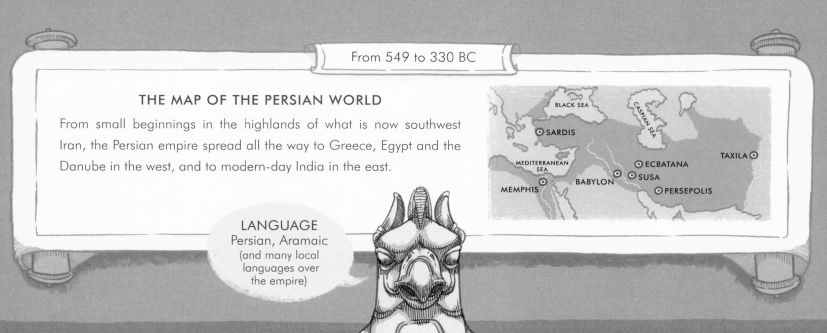

From 549 to 330 BC

### THE MAP OF THE PERSIAN WORLD

From small beginnings in the highlands of what is now southwest Iran, the Persian empire spread all the way to Greece, Egypt and the Danube in the west, and to modern-day India in the east.

BLACK SEA

CASPIAN SEA

SARDIS

TAXILA

MEDITERRANEAN SEA

ECBATANA

SUSA

BABYLON

MEMPHIS

PERSEPOLIS

**LANGUAGE**
Persian, Aramaic
(and many local languages over the empire)

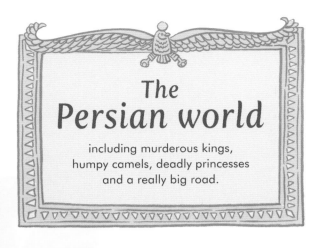

# The Persian world

including murderous kings, humpy camels, deadly princesses and a really big road.

## 1 CAMBYSES II
His dad, Cyrus, conquered most of the Middle East, which must have been a hard act to follow. Cambyses just conquered Egypt – and became pharaoh as well as king, which seems a bit greedy.

## 2 ARMY
All Persian boys had to serve in the army, but the growing empire still needed more soldiers. Kings used mercenaries from all over the place – especially for sea battles, as not many Persians could swim.

## 3 ATOSSA
Chief-wife of Darius I (he had loads of wives). She was previously married to her brother Cambyses, which seems odd, but was common at the time. Very powerful in government, she made sure her favourite son, Xerxes, became the next king.

## 4 XERXES I
Called Xerxes the Great – but his running of the empire wasn't. His army was clobbered by the Greeks, and he famously ordered the sea to be whipped after a storm destroyed his boat bridges. He then frittered away a fortune on swanky building projects.

## 5 THE ROYAL ROAD
Good roads were rare at this time. The Royal Road was well guarded and stretched over 2,400km from Sardis to Susa. Just one drawback: when Alexander the Great invaded, his army could simply stroll down the road.

## 6 CARAVANSERAIS
Inns dotted along the Royal Road. Travellers could eat, rest, feed their animals and have baths (essential after weeks travelling on a camel). People from many countries exchanged ideas, traditions, beliefs and languages here.

## 7 DARIUS I
A general who seized power when Cambyses died, and modestly called himself 'Darius the Great'. To be fair, he made the empire even bigger and created amazing new cities like Persepolis.

## 8 BARDIYA (or GAUMATA)
While Cambyses was in Egypt his brother, Prince Bardiya, stole the throne and became king . . . or did he? Some said 'Bardiya' was actually an imposter called Gaumata, who had murdered Bardiya and taken his place. Whoever he was, Darius I eventually killed him and became king instead.

## 9 CYRUS THE GREAT
According to legend when Cyrus was a baby, his grandad, who was king of the Medes, dreamed Cyrus would grow up to overthrow him. He ordered the baby to be killed, but a shepherd brought him up instead. Cyrus went on to found the Persian empire, conquering his grandad and much of the Middle East.

## 10 CASSANDANE
Cyrus' chief wife. He loved her so much (not a common feature in noble marriages of the day) that he made the whole empire go into mourning when she died.

## 11 ANGAROS
Super-fast horse-riders who carried government messages. They passed messages forward like in a relay race, and could get a message from Sardis to Susa in about a week (it took 90 days on foot).

## 12 MAGI
The name for Persian priests. It's where the English word 'magic' comes from. As well as religious duties, magi had some decidedly non-magical jobs, like checking grain stocks and supervising workers.

## 13 DATAMES
A satrap (governor of a province) and a very cunning general. He led a revolt of satraps against the king, and was a pain in the royal backside for many years.

## 14 TAXILA
One of the furthest cities in the empire, way off east in what's now Pakistan. That's one heck of a long way to ride on a horse. Couriers' hearts must have sunk when they saw 'Taxila' on a message.

## 15 ARTAXERXES I, XERXES II, SOGDIANUS, DARIUS II
A series of kings who rose (and fell) one after the other, by murdering people who got in their way. Not a great example for the children.

## 16 PERSIAN ART
The Persians specialised in intricate rock carvings, mostly showing scenes glorifying the king. Some huge ones still stand today in front of royal tombs.

## 17 BAGOAS
A powerful minister, and all-round nasty individual. He murdered King Artaxerxes III and all of his sons. He tried to poison Darius III, too – but the king made Bagoas drink the poison instead.

## 18 IMMORTALS
The elite troops of the Persian army were 10,000 soldiers called The Immortals. If one of them was wounded or killed, another soldier would immediately take his place, so the troop stayed the same size.

## 19 ROXANA
Some noble Persian ladies could fight and use weapons. Maybe Alexander the Great should've remembered that when he married three Persian princesses, Roxana, Parysatis and Stateira, as first-wife Roxana ended up killing the other two.

## 20 BABYLON
Remember Babylon in Mesopotamia? It was still powerful and famous for its hanging gardens. The Persians conquered it by diverting a river that ran alongside it. By lowering the waters they could ride over on their horses.

## 21 DARIUS III
The last ruler of the empire. He fought Alexander the Great, who defeated him, took over the title of king, plus all his lands, and even married his daughter. Ouch.

# My Kingdom *from* a Horse

## HOW DARIUS WON A CONTEST TO BECOME THE KING OF KINGS

Becoming a king is never easy, but Darius the Great did it in a particularly odd way. He was certainly a powerful noble, and one of King Cambyses' most trusted generals, but he wasn't heir to the throne.

When King Cambyses went off to conquer Egypt, Darius naturally went, too. Meanwhile, back in Persia, the king's brother, Bardiya, took advantage of their absence – and grabbed the throne for himself. This kicked off a civil war, with some people staying loyal to Cambyses, while others backed his brother.

In a further twist, some stories claim that the usurper wasn't the king's brother at all. They say it was a magus called Gaumata, who had killed Bardiya and was impersonating him. (After all, it must have been a lot easier to pass for someone else back then, with no birth certificates, photos or mobile phones.)

Eventually King Cambyses died. Darius, alongside six other nobles, led the army back from Egypt to Persia and killed Bardiya (or maybe Gaumata – who knows?)

The empire was left without a leader. Darius and the other nobles had to decide who was going to be the next king, which is a bit of an unusual situation. Normally kings inherited the throne or killed their predecessors (or both, though not in that order).

They put their heads together and came up with a plan. They'd all line up on their horses and watch the sun rise. The person whose horse was the first to react to the rising sun would become king. It was quite an odd plan. After all, being 'the-person-who-happens-to-be-sitting-on-a-horse-that-noticed-sunlight' doesn't sound like the most comprehensive set of qualifications for running an empire, but hey.

Darius had a sneaky plan of his own, though. As the sun barely peeped over the hills, one of his servants passed a hand over his horse's nose. The horse reared and neighed – and Darius became king. (The fact that he commanded a massive army might have helped settle the matter, too.)

The story got around that Darius had won the contest by treachery, but he didn't mind. In fact, he was so proud of it that he had a statue made, proclaiming he had won the crown by cleverness.

# The Roman World

## *Fighting their way to the top*

The Romans believed they were descended from Mars, the god of war, which might explain a thing or two about them. They were certainly really good at fighting, which was bad news for all their neighbours.

Fighting didn't just happen on the battlefield, either. There was nothing Romans liked better than a day out at the arena, watching gladiators clashing swords, or criminals being forced to fight to the death.

The Romans were ruthless, disciplined, competitive and very, very successful, but there was much more to them than fighting. They were extraordinary engineers, who built marvellous roads, cities and aqueducts all over their lands. They were great public speakers and

writers – they even invented the book (no one had thought of cutting pages to the same size before, and sticking them together in a cover.)

The real battle, though, was for who should rule Rome. They tried pretty much everything: kings, a republic, and a string of spectacularly murderous emperors (plus the odd good one, luckily.) But, despite this turmoil, Rome flourished for over a thousand years. At the height of the empire, it was the biggest city in the world. Fabulous temples and villas rubbed shoulders with horrible slums, and people came from all over the world to live there.

From 753 BC to 476 AD

### THE MAP OF THE ROMAN WORLD

Rome started as a bunch of little villages in central Italy. With the help of an awful lot of fighting, it grew into a huge power, conquering large chunks of Europe, north Africa and the Near East.

BRITANNIA

GAUL

ROME

CONSTANTINOPLE

CARTHAGE   GREECE

AFRICA

EGYPT

LANGUAGE
Latin
(and many other languages, all over the empire)

# 1 BOUDICA

Queen of the Iceni, a British tribe. When Boudica's husband died, the Romans pinched her land and had her flogged. Boudica fought back fiercely, leading her warriors into battle. Her name means 'victory', but sadly she lost in the end.

# 2 VERCINGETORIX

A brave warrior of Gaul (modern-day France) who led a bunch of tribes against Julius Caesar. Although he lost, he fought so cleverly that even the Romans were impressed.

# 3 HANNIBAL

The fierce leader of Carthage (a city in modern-day Tunisia). Hannibal clearly liked a challenge. He invaded Italy by riding elephants over the Alps – surely not the easiest method.

# 4 PLINY THE YOUNGER

Pliny wrote lots of long letters, which give us all sorts of fascinating details about Roman life. He famously described the eruption of Mount Vesuvius, which buried the town of Pompeii in volcanic ash.

# 5 HORTENSIA

Rome was mostly run by men, so Hortensia was very unusual in being a female orator. She gave a famous speech in the Forum, objecting to a tax on wealthy women. She couldn't see why women should be taxed to pay for men's wars.

# 6 AUGUSTUS

Rome's first emperor. Augustus took over after Julius Caesar was murdered, and ruled for over 40 years. He did such a good job the Romans named the month of August after him, and worshipped him as a god after his death.

# 7 JULIA AUGUSTA

Augustus' wife. Clever, determined and powerful, she played a big role in ruling Rome, and made sure her son Tiberius became the next emperor (whether he wanted to or not).

# 8 CATO THE YOUNGER

A gloomy senator who could bang on for hours in the Senate. He hated corruption, refused to take bribes and desperately tried to stop Julius Caesar taking over as dictator.

# 9 NERO

An emperor best known for being a bit bonkers. Did very little ruling, lots of murdering, and spent his time playing music, throwing wild parties, and even competing in the Olympic Games (where everyone sensibly let him win.)

# 10 AGRIPPINA THE YOUNGER

Nero's mum. She worked really hard to get her son into power, only to be murdered by the ungrateful little devil when he became emperor.

# 21 JULIUS CAESAR

A bold, ambitious noble who broke all the rules. After conquering lots of other people, he led his army into Rome (which was a big no-no), conquered his own people and was made 'dictator for life'. All Roman emperors after him took the name Caesar.

## 11 THE COLOSSEUM
A massive arena used for everything from gladiatorial fights to theatre. It was even flooded sometimes, to stage sea battles.

## 12 ARMINIUS
A German chieftain. Arminius originally fought in the Roman army, but when Rome started treating the German tribes badly, he switched sides. He led the Germans to a totally crushing victory and seriously wounded the Romans' pride.

## 13 CICERO
The greatest orator and writer of his day. He wrote thousands of books, essays and letters, and invented lots of new Latin words. He was a wily politician, too, but made too many enemies, and was finally executed.

## 14 EAGLE STANDARDS
These banners were considered sacred, and had to be protected at all costs in battle. When the army lost three standards to Arminius, Augustus mourned as if a family member had been killed.

The many and extensive lands of
# the Roman world
including colossal arenas, caring wolves, hot-water baths and even hotter volcanoes.

## 15 CONSTANTINE THE GREAT
The Roman empire had become so big, an earlier emperor split it in half. Constantine reunited the empire, and chose Byzantium as its new capital. He modestly renamed it Constantinople after himself. (Today it's called Istanbul.)

## 16 HORACE
One of Rome's favourite poets, and a pal of Augustus. He liked peace and quiet, and wrote (a lot) about retiring to a little farm where he could grow grapes and eat cheese all day.

## 17 SLAVES
Slaves did all the hard work in Rome. They were treated horribly, but some managed to save money and buy their freedom. A few of the most famous advisors to Roman emperors were freed slaves.

## 18 ROMULUS AND REMUS
Twin sons of Mars, the god of war. Unusually, they were suckled by a wolf when they were babies. Romulus founded Rome and was its first king. Remus was killed by his brother. Families, eh?

## 19 HYPATIA
One of the first women to study astronomy and mathematics. She built her own instruments, performed lots of experiments and ran a prestigious philosophy school.

## 20 CLEOPATRA
The pharaoh of Egypt. She had a busy life, becoming ruler at 18, killing lots of her family and having children first with Julius Caesar, then with his second-in-command, Mark Antony. She was so famous that lots of Romans copied her hairstyle.

# There's no place like Rome

## BABIES, WOLVES AND CRAZY EMPERORS

According to legend, Rome's history began when Mars, the god of war, had twin baby boys called Romulus and Remus. The boys' human mother couldn't look after them, and the babies were abandoned. Luckily, a passing she-wolf nursed them until they were adopted by a shepherd.

They grew into strong, wilful lads, and decided to found a city. Unfortunately, they had a massive argument over where to build it, and Romulus ended up killing Remus. Oops. Not a great start. (But at least Romulus got to name Rome after himself.)

Although it's a myth, this story does seem quite appropriate, as so much of Rome's history consists of ambitious plans, accompanied by an awful lot of murder.

Rome's main plan was to conquer its neighbours, starting with the bits closest to home. The Romans eventually took over every single country around the Mediterranean Sea (which was handy if they fancied a day by the seaside.) But it's not easy ruling such an enormous area.

## ALL ROADS LEAD TO ROME

Romans had a passion for engineering, and believed any problem could be solved with cleverness and a lot of hard work. Wherever the Romans went they brought new ideas with them. For instance at a time when most people were struggling to walk or ride along muddy paths and fields, the Romans built huge, reliable, paved roads linking all parts of their empire.

## THE TORTOISE OF WAR

The *testudo* (the Latin word for 'tortoise') was a battle formation in which soldiers created a solid barrier with their shields, like a tortoise shell. It was mainly used in siege battles, so the army could reach a city's wall without being boshed on the head.

For hundreds of years, Rome had been a republic, which meant people could vote to elect their leaders (well, *some* people: rich men, basically. Not women, or foreigners, or slaves or poor men.) But then Rome's leaders started fighting each other, and a noble called Julius Caesar decided it would be better if he ruled Rome all by himself. He became 'dictator for life' – but was murdered within a few months. That really set a trend.

After Caesar, Rome was ruled by a whole string of emperors, and a staggering one in five of them came to a sticky end. There was Nero, for instance, who killed his mum, his two wives, and many others. And Caligula, who had people tortured for fun, and wanted to make his horse a consul (the top job in Roman government). The horse would probably have done a better job than his master.

So how come the Roman empire was so successful for so long? Well, despite the evil, extravagant emperors, it was actually a relatively calm place to live for most of its people. And its brilliant writers, thinkers and engineers left an astonishing legacy.

Not bad for a city that started with two babies and a wolf.

## POTTY ABOUT TOILETS

Big cities produce a lot of filth, and the Romans were keen on being clean. They built enormous arched bridges called aqueducts which carried clean water to their public baths and toilets. Most Romans couldn't afford a loo at home, so public toilets had to be big – some could fit in over 100 people. They sat side by side, often having a good gossip while they did their business.

## HARD NEWS

The *Acta Diurna* (Daily Acts) were news stories carved into large stone plaques, that were put in public places for everyone to read. The stories varied from local stuff like marriages, deaths and lawsuits, to news from the provinces and war. Carving a whole newspaper every day must have been hard work – imagine if you made a mistake!

# Roman Life

## DANGEROUS GAMES

A sure way to please the Romans was to stage some games, and the more spectacular the better. Emperors even flooded whole stadia so that they could re-enact famous naval battles, complete with replica ships and sea creatures such as seals and hippos.

However, the most popular entertainment was chariot racing. It was fast, dangerous, and often produced huge crashes which killed both charioteers and horses.

Romans were a blood-thirsty lot. Another favourite sport was gladiatorial contests, in which gladiators fought, sometimes to the death, for the amusement of the crowd.

## A BIRDIE TOLD ME

Romans had some truly bonkers ways of trying to predict the future. Roman *augurs* (a type of priest) analysed the flight of birds like eagles, ravens and woodpeckers, to decide if the omens were good or bad. Another type of prophecy involved killing and disembowelling an animal, and 'reading' its entrails. Ugh.

## BIG BANQUETS

If rich Romans wanted to show off they could throw a big party with a complicated banquet. Delicacies included dormice glazed in honey and flamingo tongues. Romans also went crazy for a sauce called *garum*, made from fermented fish guts. They didn't sit down to eat, but reclined in chairs, and used their fingers instead of cutlery.

## TOGAS

Roman men had to wear a toga for formal occasions. It was an immense piece of fabric that they wore draped around themselves. Togas could be very big and heavy, so most Romans needed help to put them on. Once their togas were properly folded over (and over, and over) the wearers could barely move – which is probably why they needed slaves to do all their work.

# The Maurya World
## *Pillars of the community*

If you want to unite a bunch of little kingdoms into one big country, it helps to have nine thousand battle elephants. Luckily, Chandragupta Maurya not only had the elephants, he also had skill, determination – and a brilliant advisor who ran the new empire like a super-efficient machine.

The two of them were incredibly successful, building roads, reservoirs and temples over a vast area, from freezing mountains to steamy jungles, and governing an incredibly diverse bunch of people.

Chandragupta's grandson, Ashoka, carried on the good work in an even more radical way. Having fought lots of successful battles, he was so appalled by the carnage he'd caused that he made an extraordinary decision: he'd stop conquering any more people and focus on looking after the ones he already had. As a result, he covered the empire with messages which encouraged (well, told) people to give up violence and be good. These inscriptions were everywhere, mostly on huge stone pillars. Although their intentions were genuinely great, it must have been slightly annoying to have the architecture telling you what to do all the time.

The Mauryan empire didn't last long. After little more than a century it broke apart, but it left behind a rich legacy of culture, ideas – and big stone pillars.

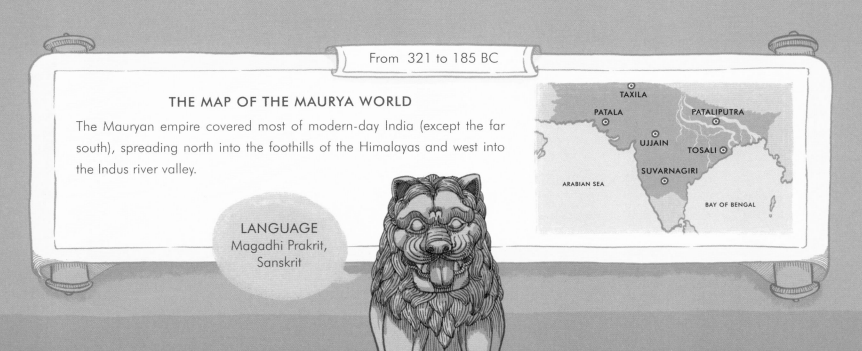

From 321 to 185 BC

### THE MAP OF THE MAURYA WORLD

The Mauryan empire covered most of modern-day India (except the far south), spreading north into the foothills of the Himalayas and west into the Indus river valley.

TAXILA
PATALA
PATALIPUTRA
UJJAIN
TOSALI
ARABIAN SEA
SUVARNAGIRI
BAY OF BENGAL

LANGUAGE
Magadhi Prakrit,
Sanskrit

**1** ASHOKA

An extraordinary emperor. He'd been a ruthless conqueror, but had a change of heart after a particularly bloody battle. He converted to a religion called Buddhism and became a model emperor, building roads and hospitals and spreading peace and good vibes throughout his empire.

**2** SANGHAMITTA

A princess who became a missionary. She begged her dad, Ashoka, to let her sail to neighbouring Sri Lanka to help her brother Mahinda with his Buddhist work. Some claim she had to fight off nagas (snake-like water spirits) on the way.

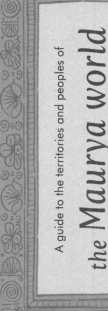

A guide to the territories and peoples of

## the Maurya world

featuring peaceful emperors, bossy pillars and fighty elephants.

### 19 DASHARATHA

He became emperor when his grandad, Ashoka, died, but struggled to keep the empire together. Lots of bits of it declared independence during his reign. His cousin, Samprati, took over after him, and managed to win some of them back.

### 20 PEACOCKS

One theory about Chandragupta Maurya is that his family tamed peacocks for a living. The Sanskrit word for peacock is mayura, which could be where 'Maurya' comes from.

### 21 KARUVAKI

A fisherman's daughter who became a queen when Ashoka fell in love with her and married her. She was proud of her charitable work, and made sure everyone read about it in edicts spread across the land.

### 3 THE BODHI TREE

A sacred fig tree under which the Buddha (founder of the Buddhist religion) meditated. Sanghamitra took a sapling from it and planted it in Sri Lanka. It's still there over 2,000 years later, making it the oldest flowering plant in the world.

### 4 ASANDHIMITRA

Ashoka's chief wife (he had five). She played an important role, advising him and helping govern the country. They were married thirty years, and he was very sad when she died.

### 5 EDICTS OF ASHOKA

Ashoka left lots of inscriptions around the empire, engraved on pillars and rocks. They're a set of rules, called edicts, in which he suggested to people (well, told them, really) how to behave.

### 6 CHANDRAGUPTA MAURYA

Ashoka's grandad, Chandragupta, created the Maurya empire by conquering lots of little kingdoms. He was a fearsome warrior and an excellent emperor. But even emperors can get tired of telling people what to do, and he eventually retired and became a monk.

### 7 PATALIPUTRA

Capital of the Maurya empire. It was one of the largest cities in the world at the time. According to Greek ambassador Megasthenes, it had 570 towers, the most beautiful palaces in the world, and tame peacocks roaming the parks.

### 8 DURDHARA

Chandragupta's wife. Her husband's advisor, Kautilya, wanted to protect him from being poisoned, so he put little doses of poison in his food, to get his body used to it. Tragically, Durdhara ate the food instead, and died.

### 9 SAMPRATI

Ashoka's grandson. Samprati eventually became emperor in place of his dad, Kunala, who had been blinded. He did a good job, building thousands of temples, and fighting to hold the empire together, as it started to fall apart.

### 10 BINDUSARA

Bindusara had the misfortune of being the son of a super-famous emperor (Chandragupta) and the dad of a mega-famous emperor (Ashoka), so no one talks about him much.

### 11 MEGASTHENES

A Greek scholar who went to the Mauryan court as an ambassador. He wrote a book describing the richness and splendour he found, and the people and places he met on his travels. He also claimed there were unicorns. Well, you can't get everything right.

### 12 BATTLE ELEPHANTS

Mauryan armies had lots of battle elephants. No one knows how effective they were, but the sight of hundreds of pachyderms in armour was usually enough to send enemies running.

### 13 SELEUCUS I NICATOR

A Greek general who became king of the lands next to the Maurya empire. 'Nicator' means 'victor', but he couldn't beat the Mauryans when he tried to invade. He eventually agreed to go away if Chandragupta gave him 500 elephants.

### 14 BRIHADRATHA

The last (and unluckiest) Mauryan emperor. The empire was much smaller by the time he inherited it. He was then murdered during a military parade by one of his generals, Pushyamitra Shunga, who started his own empire.

### 15 KUNALA

Ashoka's son. He was blinded by his jealous stepmother, who wanted to stop him becoming emperor. His son, Samprati, eventually became emperor instead.

### 16 KAUTILYA

Chandragupta's teacher and most important minister. He helped Chandragupta come to power, and set up a ferociously efficient system for running the empire (which unfortunately included spying on everyone.)

### 17 LION CAPITAL

A huge sculpture of four lions that stood on top of one of Ashoka's pillars. The four lions are still an important symbol in India today, and have become the country's official emblem.

### 18 TAXILA

Capital of one bit of the empire. You'll find this city on the Persian map, too. Being in the middle of so many places meant that poor Taxila kept getting conquered all the time.

# The Edicts of Ashoka

## HOW TO BE GOOD

Emperor Ashoka spent years fighting wars, putting down rebellions and conquering new lands, but one day he'd had enough. After a horrible campaign of conquest, during which lots of people were killed, he became so sick of seeing violence that he tried to find ways of ruling the empire *without* being violent (well, not *too* violent).

He stopped fighting unnecessary wars and made many improvements to benefit his subjects. One of the most memorable things he created were his edicts.

He put inscriptions all over the empire – usually on huge stone pillars or carved on rocks – explaining how people should behave and do good in the world. They were written in different languages so that everyone could read them (some were even written in Greek). They were quite long, but here are some of the main themes.

*Trees should be planted and wells dug around roads, so men and cattle can rest.*

*No living being should be killed or sacrificed.*

*Respect all elders, parents and teachers.*

*Kindness is the greatest virtue.*

*All people should be treated well.*

*Looking for glory and fame is not good.*

*All religions should be tolerated.*

*There is merit in owning and spending little.*

# Mauryan Life

## STUNNING STUPAS

*Stupa* means 'heap' in Sanskrit, but these huge temples are much more than that. They're shaped like burial mounds, and were built to store Buddhist relics (usually the remains of dead people). Emperor Ashoka built thousands, putting some ashes from the Buddha himself inside each one. His Great Stupa at Sanchi is one of the biggest in the world, and is decorated with beautiful carvings.

## THE GOOD EMPIRE GUIDE

The *Arthashastra* is a book written by Kautilya, Chandragupta's chief advisor. It gives tons of detailed information on how to run a huge empire, covering everything from war and spying to when the emperor should murder members of his family. Less horridly, it also says that the emperor should work hard to ensure the happiness of his people.

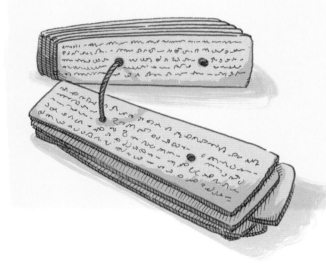

## CURIOUS COINS

Mauryan coins were very different from the little round things we have today. They were called punch-marked coins: little flattened lumps of silver in all sorts of shapes, embossed with symbols. The coins' weight determined their value.

## DON'T FLASH YOUR CASH

Mauryan rulers were a bit too fond of spying on their subjects. Even Ashoka, who was so concerned with doing good, had a huge network of spies spread all around the country. They didn't spy on enemies, though, but on regular folk. Having too much money was considered a bad thing (unless you were the emperor, of course), so the spies would report anyone that became a bit too flashy.

# TUCK IN!

A selection of surprising and delectable dishes
from past times and places

## STARTERS

### *Wolf Soup*
Soup made from roasted wolf leg, onions and spices. Very popular with Mongol emperors.
Why eat a sheep when you can eat a huge carnivorous beast?

### *Beaver's Tail*
Traditionally, some Christians don't eat meat during certain religious holidays, only fish. As beavers spend a lot of
time in water, people decided they counted as fish, and could be eaten on holy days. Poor beavers.

## MAINS

### *Songbird Pie*
A showstopper pie at royal banquets in the Middle Ages in Europe. Luckily, the songbirds were put in
the pie *after* it was baked so that, when it was cut open, they could fly out and sing.

### *Roasted Human*
Throughout history, some peoples have eaten other people, mostly as part of ritual sacrifice, or during wars. Although we
(apparently) taste like pork, eating people has never been a popular option. These days it's definitely frowned on.

##  DESSERT

### *Hairy Caramel*
Caramel wasn't invented to be eaten. Melted sugar was first
used in the ancient Middle East as a way to remove body hair.
Finally someone tried it and found it tasted excellent
(hopefully *before* using it to remove their hair.)

### *Medicinal Candy*
Candy made out of cane sugar was first sold in Europe in the
18th century AD. It was taken as medicine, and only very rich
people could afford it. Just as well, since it wouldn't have
made anyone better – maybe just cheered them up a bit.

##  DRINKS

### *Bitter Chocolate*
Originally, chocolate was only consumed in Central
and South America. The Aztecs made a bitter drink from
cocoa beans, which they called *chocolatl*.

### *Tasty Tea*
Chinese monks used to drink tea as part of their
meditation rituals. Eventually people all round the world
discovered how great tea was. It was healthy, too, as
boiling the water killed any bugs.

# The Tang World

## *Poetry, murder and a nice cup of tea*

Welcome to China's golden age. Prepare to be dazzled by fabulous art, elegant poetry, dramatic acrobatics and astonishing technology. Yes, China was pretty much the most advanced civilisation in the world at this time. Under the Tang rulers, the Chinese developed everything from paper-making and book printing to gunpowder and clocks. They even made tea the national drink, and you can't get more civilised than that.

The Tang emperors, meanwhile, had the tricky task of running a massive country, while trying not to be murdered by their family. In one way they were lucky: when they took over, China was already one of the biggest nations on earth, so they didn't have to waste time conquering lots of other people.

On the down side, the whole country was bristling with plots and intrigues. The emperors were kept busy squashing one rebellion after another, and that's what finished them off in the end.

When the Tang first took over, the country was in chaos after years of war. It took a while to settle things down but, when they finally did, the Tang created some pretty extraordinary stuff. Tang poetry is still hugely admired today, and some of their laws remained in use right up to the 20th century.

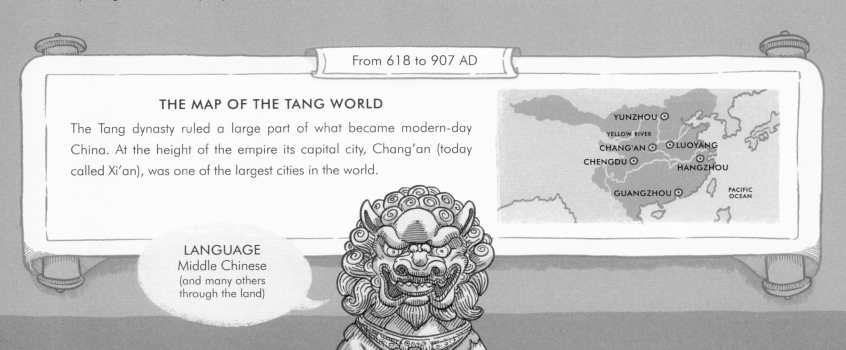

From 618 to 907 AD

### THE MAP OF THE TANG WORLD

The Tang dynasty ruled a large part of what became modern-day China. At the height of the empire its capital city, Chang'an (today called Xi'an), was one of the largest cities in the world.

YUNZHOU
YELLOW RIVER
CHANG'AN · LUOYANG
CHENGDU · HANGZHOU
GUANGZHOU
PACIFIC OCEAN

**LANGUAGE**
Middle Chinese
(and many others
through the land)

**1 GAOZU**
Also called the Duke of Tang. He didn't like the way the emperors of the Sui dynasty were running things, so he organised rebellions and seized power for himself, becoming the first Tang emperor.

**2 GOLD FISH**
Carp are usually grey, but the Tang bred super-colourful ones, which they kept as pets in beautiful water gardens. Only emperors were allowed to keep golden carp, which seems a bit greedy.

**3 ZHU WEN**
A Tang governor and general who went very, very bad. He murdered the emperor and most of his sons, ending the Tang dynasty. He then made himself emperor – until his own son murdered him. Fun times.

**4 CHANG'AN**
The empire's western capital. Its name means 'Perpetual Peace', but that didn't stop it being almost destroyed during a rebellion. One of its most impressive buildings was a 330-foot tall temple called a pagoda, built to store one of the Buddha's teeth.

**5 GAOZONG AND EMPRESS WU**
When Emperor Gaozong died, his wife, Empress Wu, deposed her own son and seized power, becoming the only woman ever to rule China. Like many rulers, she stayed in power by killing thousands of people. Unlike many rulers, she actually ran the country rather well.

## 6 DAMING PALACE
The imperial palace complex in Chang'an was huge, with parks, lakes, temples, an archery hall, polo ground, football field, and troupes of singers, dancers and actors.

## 7 XUANZONG
Also called 'Illustrious August'. Ruled for over 40 years, whilst also writing music and poetry. A good emperor – yay! Oh, but then he fell in love with his son's wife, totally messed things up and eventually had to abdicate. Ah, well. You can't have it all.

## 8 MANDARINS
Not oranges, but very important government officials. They did most of the hard work of running the country, looking after everything from taxation to sewage. All the fun stuff.

## 9 YANG GUIFEI
One of the most beautiful women in China. Emperor Xuanzong fell in love with her, but she was already married . . . to his own son. To get round this tricky fact, Xuanzong made her become a nun for a bit, but then married her anyway (no, I can't keep up, either).

## 10 LI BAI AND DU FU
Poets and friends, their poems are still famous and read all across modern-day China. Legend has it that Li Bai drowned when he fell out of a boat, while trying to grasp the reflection of the moon.

## 11 CARNIVALS
If emperors felt generous, they'd give lots of food, drink and entertainment to the people. Enormous floats shaped like all manner of fantastic things paraded down the streets carrying musicians and acrobats.

## 12 HUANG CHAO
Huang was well educated, but failed his civil-service exams. He took to smuggling salt (as you do), and later became a fearsome rebel leader, commanding one of the forces that brought down the Tang. If only he'd passed those exams.

## 13 BOATS
One of the best ways to get about Tang China was by boat. Some boats were more like floating houses or palaces, complete with multiple storeys and even tiled roofs.

## 14 ZHONGZONG AND WEI
Zhongzong was the son of Empress Wu. He became emperor briefly, but his wife, Wei, wanted to rule as well. He ended up being deposed by his mum and poisoned to death by his wife. Embarrassing.

## 15 PRINCESS ANLE
Zhongzong and Wei's favourite daughter. She and her sisters weren't exactly models of good behaviour. Some of their favourite activities were stealing, selling favours, enslaving people and building extravagant mansions.

## 16 DEZONG
An emperor who ruled successfully for over 20 years, despite having to put down one rebellion after another. He'd probably rather have been a poet – he even sent orders to his ministers in verse.

## 17 THE GREAT WALL
The Chinese do seem to like a good wall. Most of the Great Wall of China was built later, during the Ming dynasty. However, walls had been built on the northern frontier for hundreds of years to protect the empire from invasion.

## 18 ZHANG XU
The Tang loved calligraphy – the art of posh handwriting. They considered it as important as poetry or music. Zhang was the most famous calligrapher of his time. (He also became famous for being drunk all the time, but that's a lot less impressive.)

## 19 CLOTHES
Flash clothes showed off how grand you were. One princess wore a dress made from feathers of over a hundred different birds. People were very impressed. Birds probably weren't.

## 20 AN LUSHAN
A powerful general. He was a favourite of Emperor Xuanzong's – until he organised a massive rebellion and made himself emperor. Talk about ingratitude. Millions died in the process and Xuanzong abdicated. All in all, a pretty nasty business.

An interpretation of

# the Tang world

featuring spectacular cities, poetic emperors and inedible mandarins.

# Tang Cleverness
## BENDING OVER BACKWARDS TO ENTERTAIN YOU

Tang emperors certainly knew how to throw a massive party. All over the country, they'd give people time off work, serve them humongous feasts and stage impressive parades. Things were particularly extraordinary in the capital, with floats that looked like huge mobile mountains and giant ships. As if that wasn't enough, there was also entertainment from musicians, magicians and especially acrobats, some of whom did amazing (if slightly foolhardy) things like climbing ladders made from swords or balancing lots of other people on their heads. Seriously, don't try that at home.

## THINGS THAT GO BOOM

The Tang could make a party go with a bang – literally. One of their most important inventions was gunpowder, from which they made fireworks. (They hadn't yet worked out that they could also use it to make horrible weapons.) Surprisingly, it was philosophers who first created gunpowder, in an attempt to make a potion of immortality. Unsurprisingly, they had some very nasty accidents along the way.

## WOOD-BLOCK PRINTING

At a time when almost everyone else was still laboriously copying books out by hand, the Tang worked out how to print multiple copies of books using wood-block printing. The words and pictures were carved on pieces of wood, then covered in ink and pressed on to paper. Good news for authors who wanted to become famous. Probably rather bad news for scribes.

## CLEVER COGS

The Tang were excellent at making all sorts of machines using gears and cogs. They invented a variety of clocks, and loads of helpful machines that did things they presumably couldn't be bothered to do themselves, from ringing bells to hitting drums. They especially liked automata — intricate moving statues that could perform handy tasks like pouring wine into cups.

## TERRIFIC TESTS

The Advanced Scholars Examination was a really tricky exam that people had to pass to get a job in the civil service. It involved learning classic texts off by heart and even writing poetry — not the most obvious skill for running a country, but it must have made the office correspondence more fun to read.

# Tang Sporting Life

Sports were very popular in Tang China. Most people, from emperors to farmers, loved watching and practising all sorts of games. Surprisingly, some sports that we play today, like football and polo, were also popular in Tang China. Unusually for the time, most sports were practised by women as well as men. Mind you, not all their sports are so familiar to us. Ever tried hunting wolves using eagles? Nope, didn't think so.

## KEEPY-UPPY

The Chinese had been playing versions of football for centuries and, by the time of the Tang, there were playing fields all over Chang'an. One version was very similar to the one we play today, with two sides trying to score goals. Individual players could also show off by trying to keep the ball in the air without dropping it – these days we'd call it 'keepy-uppy'.

## CLIP-CLOP-BONK

Tang nobles loved playing a game very similar to polo. They rode on horseback (and sometimes on *donkeyback*), using long sticks to hit balls and score goals. It was such a popular game that nobles were often buried alongside pottery figures of polo horses and polo players.

## SHARP SHOOTERS

Archery was not only a sport, it was also a very useful military skill. Ancient Chinese archers learned to shoot in all sorts of positions, but the most impressive by far was shooting while riding a horse. It was such a prized skill that state officials were required to be good shots in order to have a chance of getting a job.

# The Mongol World
## *One giant steppe for mankind*

It's easy to be a Mongol conqueror: you just have to be able to wield a weapon in each hand while steering a horse with your knees. You also have to keep on the move, carrying your home from place to place. For a long time, that's how Mongols lived: as nomadic tribes, galloping about the enormous grasslands north of China, living in tents and boshing one another.

Then along came Genghis Khan: a brilliant, ruthless leader who stopped them fighting each other, and got them conquering other people instead. Before long, Genghis and his Mongol warriors had clobbered everyone into submission from China to the edge of Europe.

The Mongols are often dismissed as murderous barbarians (and they certainly killed a staggering number of people – some say over 35 million.) However, other civilisations could be just as bloodthirsty, and Mongol culture was sophisticated in lots of unique ways. As nomads, they didn't need sculptors, architects and stonemasons. They loved art, though, and eagerly employed talented craftspeople in every country they conquered. They even built great cities across their empire.

So was life under the Mongols that bad? Not necessarily – as long as you surrendered quickly, and didn't try and put up a fight.

From 1206 to 1368 AD

### THE MAP OF THE MONGOL WORLD
At its height, the Mongol empire spread from the Yellow Sea in the east all the way to the borders of modern-day Hungary in the west.

KIEV
MOSCOW
VOLGA RIVER
KARAKORUM
BAGHDAD
SAMARKAND
KHANBALIQ
YELLOW SEA
YANGTZE RIVER

LANGUAGE
Mongolian
(and many other
languages)

# 1 GENGHIS KHAN

The big daddy of the Mongolian empire. His name, rather modestly, means 'Ruler of the Universe'. He didn't quite conquer the universe (that would be tricky on a horse), but he did bring roughly a quarter of the world's people under Mongol rule.

# 2 KHULAN KHATUN

One of Genghis Khan's many wives (he had more than ten). Khulan must have been pretty intrepid, as she was the only wife who rode with him into battle.

# 3 THE SILK ROAD

Merchants used this ancient route to carry all sorts of goods to and from Europe – silks, spices, gold, you name it. It had been plagued by bandits, but the Mongols soon sorted them out and made it safe.

# 4 SPIES

The Mongols' favourite way of conquering cities wasn't violent, it was super clever. They sent spies on ahead to spread the word about what horrors awaited if the citizens tried to put up a fight. Most people surrendered straightaway.

# 5 ÖGEDEI KHAN

Genghis Khan's son. He expanded his dad's empire all the way to Europe. Clever, popular and even quite humble (for an emperor), he was also a bit of a drunkard, and that finished him off in the end.

# 6 SORGHAGHTANI BEKI

Wife of one of Genghis' sons – and one of the most powerful people in the empire. Two of her sons became emperors. She couldn't read, but she made sure her sons could – and made them learn the languages of the peoples they conquered.

# 7 QUTULUN KHATUN

The daughter of a rebel chieftain. Qutulun was a great warrior. She challenged anyone who wanted to marry her to a wrestling match, and made them wager 100 horses. She beat so many suitors, they say she won more than 10,000 horses.

# 8 YURTS

Mongol tents were more like buildings. There were even yurt palaces which were so big they couldn't be taken apart. They were placed on wheels and pulled by oxen. Servants could even cook dinner inside while on the move.

# 9 BÖRTE FUJIN

Genghis Khan's chief wife and Great Empress. They got engaged when he was 9 years old, which seems a tad early. Like many Mongol empresses, Börte ruled over her own lands. She also helped run the empire when Genghis was at war (which was a lot).

# 10 KARAKORUM

Genghis Khan's original capital city. It had some grand buildings, but also areas where people could pitch their yurts. They were nomads, after all.

# 11 TÖREGENE KHATUN

Ögedei's wife. A remarkable character who, when her husband died, took over and ran the empire for five years. She even appointed another woman, Fatima, as her chief advisor.

## 12 GÜYÜK KHAN
Son of Ögedei and Töregene. His mum made sure he got the job of emperor, even though he wasn't Ögedei's heir, but then she didn't let him rule. She did the job herself, which must have been embarrassing for him.

## 13 FAITHFUL ADVISORS
It's tricky ruling people with so many different religious beliefs. Mongol emperors had all sorts of religious advisors, from Muslim imams and Christian priests to Buddhist monks and shamans.

## 14 KURULTAI
Mongol emperors could choose their heir, but their choice had to be confirmed by the chiefs of all the tribes at a lively gathering called a *kurultai*.

## 15 SUBUTAI
The son of a blacksmith who rose to be a brilliant (and slightly terrifying) military leader. He won hundreds of battles for the emperors. Surprisingly, after all that, he retired and died peacefully of old age.

## 16 TSA-CHÜ OPERA
A form of Chinese theatre that became popular under Kublai Khan. Lead actresses in *Tsa-Chü* operas became incredibly famous, but they also had to sing more than 40 songs in a row. Let's hope they were short songs.

## 17 MARCO POLO
An Italian merchant who travelled to China and became a pal of Kublai Khan's. He was super-impressed by the splendour of Kublai's court. On his return to Italy, he wrote a book about his travels which became a smash hit across Europe.

## 18 KUBLAI KHAN
Genghis Khan's grandson. His greatest achievement was the conquest of China, and even the Chinese reckoned he did a pretty good job of ruling it. Among other things, Kublai's credited with making everyone in China use paper money.

## 19 KHANBALIQ
This was the Mongol capital city under Kublai Khan. It's in China, and today it's called Beijing.

A map of the many conquered lands of

# the Mongol world

with speedy horses, huge tents and lots of singing.

## 20 ARIK BÖKE
Kublai Khan's brother, and arch rival. He reckoned Kublai was getting a bit soft, settling down in China and giving up the nomadic Mongol lifestyle, so he fought him tooth and nail for the throne. But Kublai wasn't that soft, and Arik lost.

# Only Genghis Can

## A MAN WHO DID SO MUCH THAT HE DESERVES HIS OWN PAGE IN HISTORY (TWO PAGES, IN THIS CASE)

Founding an empire is no small feat, but Genghis Khan had a pretty extraordinary life even before he conquered a massive chunk of the world. The life of a Mongol nomad was already rather eventful, and Genghis' life was more eventful than most.

His name at birth was Temüjin, which means 'made of iron' or 'really headstrong' (which he clearly was). His dad was a noble and the leader of a nomadic tribe.

His parents decided who young Temüjin would marry when he was just a child. He went to live with his bride-to-be's family when he was nine years old. They didn't have to wait long for the wedding: in those days Mongols got married when they turned twelve.

His dad was poisoned by a rival tribe. Temüjin wanted to become chief of his tribe, so he, er . . . killed his brother (it seems to have been a pretty standard way of getting rid of unwanted competition at the time.)

After losing lots of battles, Temüjin finally got the knack of winning. He became so good at it that, eventually, all the nomadic tribes met in a *kurultai* and elected him their leader. He changed his name to Genghis Khan, which means 'ruler of the universe'. It probably seemed a little big-headed at the time, but turned out to be sort of right in the end.

The Mongol tribes had been wasting all their energy fighting each other. When Genghis took charge, he set them fighting other enemies instead. For the next twenty years he commanded Mongol armies to conquer countless other peoples.

He kept up his military campaigns till he died at the age of 65 – a ripe old age if you've spent your life riding horses at full speed with people throwing all manner of weapons at you. By that time he had been married to his first wife, Börte, for 53 years. (He was also married to lots and lots of other wives.)

Genghis wanted to be buried without any markers. That's unusual for an emperor – look at the pharaohs and their pyramids. It means no one knows where his grave is.

# Mongol Life

The Mongols were nomads, which means they didn't live in permanent cities. Instead they moved around, taking their animals from one part of the country to another, depending on the seasons. This different lifestyle meant that the Mongols developed lots of unusual ways of doing things.

## BLAZING SADDLES

Mongols were astonishing horse riders. They could stand on the saddle, and control a horse without using their hands (which were usually holding weapons). They could even do acrobatics on horseback. Most Mongol children started learning to ride at the same time as they learned how to walk.

## HUNTING HIGH AND LOW

Hunting's important if you live in the open, both to provide food and to protect you. Some Mongol tribes weren't content with just using bows and arrows or a dog. Instead they used golden eagles to swoop down on their prey.

## SING ALONG, ALONG

Mongols have a very complex way of singing called 'throat singing'. Most people can only sing one note at a time. Mongol throat-singers can sing several all at once, by training really hard to control their throat and diaphragm muscles. It's a bit like one person making all the sounds a group of people would make.

## PINS AND NEEDLES

Mongols were keen to learn from the people they conquered. In China, they learned a type of medicine called acupuncture in which a doctor pushes thin needles into specific points on your body to relieve pain. There was also a version where small bundles of herbs were set on fire over you. Both types are still very popular around the world today.

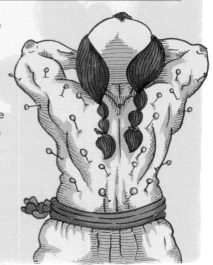

# The Ottoman World

## *Otta-way to do it*

Who would have guessed that one small Turkish tribe could create a massive empire that lasted 600 years? Probably not Osman, the chap who started it all, back in the 13th century.

The clever thing about the Ottomans was that, as they conquered more and more *and more* people, they didn't force them to change their lifestyle. Instead they welcomed the different cultures and religions into their empire. Ottoman emperors (called sultans) had queens and concubines from eastern Europe and Russia. They had Viking guards, and an army of slaves from all over the world. It made for a vibrant, exciting melting pot, and meant that the Ottomans benefited from the best art, music, architecture and ideas of everyone under their rule.

There were downsides, of course (there always are). The sultans didn't want anyone challenging them so, for hundreds of years, they executed all of their brothers, and even their brothers' sons. That no doubt kept things tidy, but it must have made for some strained family gatherings.

With absolute power, the sultans could lead a fabulously wealthy and luxurious life. We have the Ottomans to thank for all manner of lovely, civilised things like exotic tulips and beautiful carpets (and some rather less civilised things, like oil wrestling.)

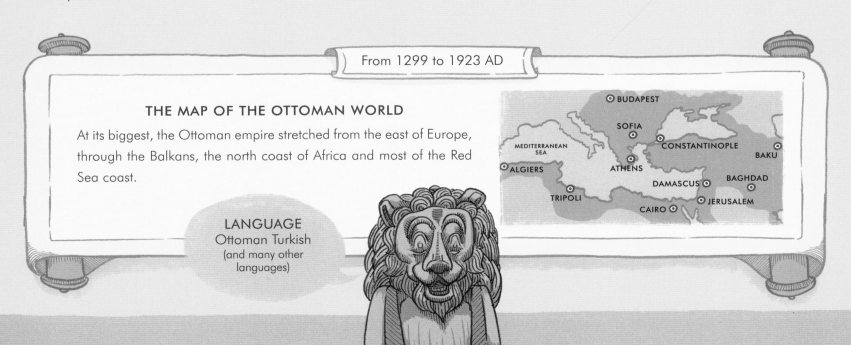

From 1299 to 1923 AD

### THE MAP OF THE OTTOMAN WORLD

At its biggest, the Ottoman empire stretched from the east of Europe, through the Balkans, the north coast of Africa and most of the Red Sea coast.

LANGUAGE
Ottoman Turkish
(and many other
languages)

**1  OSMAN**
Founder of the Ottoman dynasty. (The word 'Ottoman' comes from his name.) He was a great leader who treated absolutely everyone equally – not many rulers do that. Died of gout, which seems a bit of a let-down after such a grand life.

**2  JANISSARIES**
The sultan's personal army. All the soldiers were originally slaves, usually kidnapped from their families as children. They were highly trained, well paid and commanded great respect. (It helped that they carried big guns.)

**3  BUHURIZADE MUSTAFA ITRI**
A great musician and singer who played at the court of five different sultans. His music is still very popular today.

**4  WHIRLING DERVISHES**
A religious order of Islam in which the prayers are performed as a type of dance. Dervishes can spin around for hours without getting dizzy, which is pretty clever.

**5  TAQI AL-DIN**
One of the greatest scientists in Ottoman history. A philosopher, mathematician, astronomer, engineer, inventor – and probably a very tired man.

**6  CONSTANTINOPLE**
The Ottomans nabbed their capital city from the Romans, and made it even more magnificent. Today it's called Istanbul.

**7  MEHMED THE CONQUEROR**
The sultan who conquered Constantinople (and much, much more). Impressively, he also found time to build palaces, start a university and organise the government.

**8  KÖSEM SULTAN**
Few women got to rule the Ottoman empire, but Kösem did it three times. Two of her sons became emperor when very young, so she ruled the empire for them. The same thing happened with her grandson. After she died, she was called 'Magnificent Mother'.

**9  THE IMPERIAL HAREM**
Home of the sultans' concubines. Concubines were slaves, and were a bit like wives, except the sultans didn't marry them. Sultans had lots of children, but would only have one son with each concubine.

**10  MIMAR SINAN**
Suleiman's chief architect. He started as a humble stonemason, but went on to design many fabulous buildings. His tallest towers were 70 metres high (that's like 24 elephants stacked on top of each other.)

## AHMED KARAHISARI

The Ottomans loved calligraphy (the art of fancy writing). It took many years to train, and Ahmed was one of the very best. He created many beautiful books for the sultans.

## 11 TOPKAPI PALACE

The sultans' palace was like a small town. It had state rooms, the Harem, beautiful gardens, Turkish baths, the fabulous imperial jewel collection – and a tower from which the sultan could keep an eye on everyone.

## 13 TULIPS

These flowers were so insanely expensive, they became a symbol of wealth and power. Sultans threw a big party each year when they bloomed.

## 14 SULEIMAN THE MAGNIFICENT

This super-famous sultan expanded the empire to the max, built astonishing buildings, wrote poetry, had loads of kids – and probably never slept.

## 15 HÜRREM SULTAN

A slave in Suleiman's harem. The sultan loved her so much that he married her (which was unheard of) and let her have lots of sons (other concubines only had one son each.) She became so famous, artists came from all over the world to paint her.

## 16 MIHRIMAH SULTAN

Hürrem and Suleiman's daughter. Clearly her dad's favourite, she became his advisor and travelled everywhere with him. Better still, he didn't have her strangled (unlike her brother Mustafa).

## 17 ABDULCELIL LEVNI

A great artist who liked making very tiny paintings. He became famous for illustrating books and miniatures showing life at the sultan's court.

## 18 CARPETS

The Ottomans were world famous for making beautiful carpets. The sultans' palaces were covered with them, which must have been comfy – especially as you had to take your shoes off when you stepped inside.

## 19 MEHTERAN

The Janissaries' very own military band. The Mehteran played for them every time they went to war. It must have been quite cheering (as long as you like marching-band music, and don't mind war.)

## 20 SUPER-CANNONS

The Ottomans created absolutely massive guns to use in sieges. One cannon weighed over 16 tonnes. Pity the people who had to lug it around.

## 21 BUDA

Capital of the kingdom of Hungary. The Ottomans captured it after a long, horrible siege – then built lots of thermal public baths in it, and introduced Hungarians to coffee and a spice called paprika.

## 22 SELIM III

As well as being sultan, Selim was an excellent musician and composer. Some of his music is still popular today in Turkey. Sadly, Selim himself wasn't so popular, and was murdered by some guards during a civil war.

A presentation of the glittering cities of

# the Ottoman world

featuring comfy carpets, exotic tulips and massive cannons.

# Ottoman Life

## JUST CALL ME MEHMED

Rulers love having fancy names, and few came fancier than the titles of the Ottoman sultans. They included pretty much every single place the sultan (or his ancestors) had ever taken over – which, as you can see, was quite a long list. No doubt this made the sultans feel wonderfully grand, but spare a thought for the people who had to listen to all this every time he was introduced.

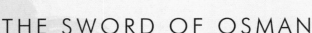

## THE SWORD OF OSMAN

When Osman I came to power, he was given a special gift: a beautiful sword covered in gold and precious jewels. From then on, receiving the sword became the most important part of a new Ottoman sultan's coronation. Thousands of people would come to watch the girding ceremony (that's what having a sword strapped on is called.)

## KIRKPINAR OIL WRESTLING

Wrestling is a very old sport, and wrestling whilst slathered in oil was popular in lots of cultures, from ancient Egypt to classical Greece and Rome. In the Ottoman empire it became a huge craze. Ottoman soldiers organised an oil-wrestling competition in the 14th century, in a place called Kirkpinar. Astonishingly, it has happened every single year since.

Sultan Mehmed Han, Sovereign of The Sublime House of Osman, Sultan of Sultans, Khan of the Khans, Commander of the faithful and Successor of the Prophet of the lord of the Universe, Custodian of the Holy Cities of Mecca, Medina and Jerusalem, Caesar of Rome, Padishah of The Three Cities of Constantinople, Edirne and Bursa, and of the Cities of Damascus and Cairo, of all Azerbaijan, of the Maghreb, of Barkah, of Kairouan of Alep, of the Arab and Persian Iraq, of Basra, of El Hasa strip, of Raqqa, of Mosul, of Parthia, of Diyar-ı Bekr, of Cilicia, of the provinces of Erzurum, of Sivas, of Adana, of Karaman, of Van, of Barbaria, of Abyssinia, of Tunisia, of Tripoli, of Syria, of Cyprus, of Rhodes, of Crete, of the province of the Peloponnese, of the Mediterranean Sea, of the Black Sea, of Anatolia, of Rumelia, of Baghdad, of Kurdistan, of Greece, of Turkestan, of Tartary, of Circassia, of the two regions of Kabarda, of Georgia, of the steppe of Kipchaks, of the whole country of the Tatars, of Theodosia and of all the neighbouring regions of Bosnia, of the City and Fort of Belgrade, of the province of Serbia, with all the castles and cities of all Arnaut, of all Wallachia and Moldavia, as well as all the dependencies and borders, and many other...

# The Inca World
## *Ruling high and low*

Fancy living like an Inca? You'd have to get used to doing a lot of things very differently. For a start, stop reading this book. The Incas didn't use an alphabet to write. Instead, they created a completely unique way of keeping records using knotted strings.

And you couldn't use money to pay for things. Incas paid each other by doing work, or swapping stuff like food, gold, beautiful fabrics or even exotic feathers. You couldn't swan about in a carriage, either, as they didn't have wheeled vehicles.

You'd have to get used to some nasty stuff, like human sacrifice. And you'd have to treat the Inca emperor like a god. He was called

*Sapa Inca*, which means 'The Only Inca', and owned *everything* that all his people produced.

Over a hundred years, the Incas built an extraordinary empire, with amazing cities, enormous temples and incredible mountain roads. A mere 40,000 of them conquered a huge part of South America, and ended up ruling millions of people. But then, very suddenly, it was all over.

Invaders arrived from Spain, bringing fancy weaponry and a bunch of devastating European diseases. In just a few years, the Incas and their empire were swept away.

From the early 1400s to 1533 AD

### THE MAP OF THE INCA WORLD

The Inca empire occupied most of South America west of the Andes mountains, from the jungles of modern-day Ecuador, all the way south into Chile and Argentina. The empire was divided into four parts, with Cuzco, the capital, at its centre.

QUITO

CHAN CHAN

PACHACAMAC · CUZCO
NAZCA · LAKE TITICACA
TIWANAKU

PACIFIC OCEAN

TALCA

**LANGUAGE**
Quechua
(and over 30 other
local languages)

# the Inca world

An annotated illumination of

including cloudy mountains, sacred lakes, mountain fortresses and grumpy llamas.

**1 CAPAC YUPANQUI**
An emperor who had a swanky new palace built, and started quite a trend. Every emperor after that wanted a new palace. At least it kept the local builders busy.

**2 MANCO CAPAC**
Founder of the Incas. Legend has it he was the son of Inti, the Incas' sun god, and that he used a magical golden staff to choose the right spot to build the city of Cuzco. True? Probably not, but it's a nice story.

**3 HUAYNA CAPAC**
An emperor who spent most of his reign trekking around the empire, making sure people paid their taxes and didn't rebel. Whoever said being an emperor was easy?

**4 LLAMAS**
Llamas may look like they're laughing at you, but they're very handy animals. The Incas used them for everything: transport, wool, meat. Even their poo made excellent fertilizer.

**5 WARRIORS**
Inca warriors reckoned that, if they were going to die, they might as well do it in style. They went into battle wearing some of their best clothes and jewellery (as well as armour and weapons – they weren't daft.)

**6 MAYTA CAPAC**
The emperor who really kick-started the Inca empire. He liked fighting as a kid, and liked it even more as a grown-up, picking fights with neighbouring peoples and doing a lot of conquering.

**7 FRANCISCO PIZARRO**
Leader of the Spanish invaders. With only a tiny army, he polished off the Inca empire, killing thousands with powerful weapons and deadly European diseases like smallpox.

**8 ATAHUALPA**
Brother of Huáscar (the fella down in the cage). Scarily, he had a cloak made from vampire bats. He beat Huáscar to become emperor, but was imprisoned by the Spanish invaders. Atahualpa offered them a whole roomful of gold and silver. The Spanish took the loot – then executed him anyway.

**9 CUZCO**
Capital of the empire and centre of the world in Inca religion. It was apparently shaped like a puma, with a fortress as the head and two rivers joining to form the tail.

**10 MACHU PICCHU**
A personal estate built for Emperor Pachacuti. He came here to escape the busy city life of Cuzco, in the calm and solitude that you can only get with 800 servants running round you.

**11 CORICANCHA**
The Temple of the Sun in Cuzco. It housed the mummified bodies of past Inca rulers, dressed in all sorts of finery. The mummies even had a zoo-garden of gold and silver plants and animals (but they couldn't stroll in it because they were dead.)

**12 FOOD AND FARMING**
It's not easy growing crops on steep mountains. The Incas had to build massive terraces, surrounded by canals. They also worked out how to freeze-dry meat and potatoes, to preserve them through the winter.

**13 PACHACUTI**
An emperor whose name means 'earth-shaker'. He certainly shook things up. He rebuilt the city of Cuzco; made sun-worship the official religion, and imposed heavy taxes on everyone. (That last one probably wasn't so popular.)

**14 MUMMIES**
The mummified bodies of some important people were kept in palaces and temples, fully dressed and sometimes even attended by live servants. That's a real dead-end job.

**15 HIGH ROADS**
The Incas built amazing roads that snaked round mountain peaks. They used rope bridges to cross over gorges.

**16 PRIESTS AND SACRIFICE**
Incas worshipped lots of gods. Their priests (men and women alike) were very powerful. They led a huge winter festival where they tried to please the sun god, Inti, by sacrificing everything from humans to guinea pigs.

**17 LAKE TITICACA**
The Incas believed the sun and moon had been born in this lake, so they built temples for them on islands.

**18 TUPAC INCA YUPANQUI**
Pachacuti's son. Called 'the Unforgettable One'. (What do you mean, you'd forgotten him?) A fearless military leader, he did a serious amount of conquering, and won a bitter war against the powerful Chimú people.

**19 CHOSEN WOMEN**
Some women were chosen to live separately, weaving and making chicha (an alcoholic drink) for the chief Inca's family. To make chicha, they chewed up corn kernels, then spat the pulp into warm water and left it to ferment. Yum!

**20 MINCHANÇAMAN**
Last ruler of the Chimú kingdom. He was so busy conquering his own neighbours, he must have been a bit surprised when the Incas conquered him back. Very popular in those days, conquering.

**21 COYAS**
Inca queens. Inca emperors married more than one woman, and their wives were clearly important, helping run the empire and giving their husbands advice.

**22 MEMORISERS**
With no written language, Incas recorded things in different ways. One way was having official memorisers: people whose job was, literally, to remember stuff.

**23 HUÁSCAR**
One of Huayna Capac's sons. He fought his brother, Atahualpa, over who should become emperor. Atahualpa won. He imprisoned Huáscar, then had him killed. Kids, eh?

# Very Important Ancestors

## MEET MY MUMMY

Most peoples from the Andes mountains worshipped their ancestors. That doesn't mean they thought their grandparents were really cool (although I'm sure they did think that, too), but that they treated the dead and their remains as sacred.

The Incas mummified the bodies of dead people (especially if the dead person was important) by drying them out in the cold climate of the Andes mountains. Once the mummies were nice and dry, they were dressed in expensive clothes and jewellery and placed in sacred places.

The mummies of dead Inca emperors were extra-special. They lived in grand rooms inside the temple of Inti, the sun god, in Cuzco. On special days the mummies would be paraded around town on litters. People would sing songs about the awesome things the mummies had done during their lives, and even feed them treats.

Mummies of dead rulers also served as messengers between the living and the gods. So if the current, non-dead emperor wanted to ask the gods about something, all he had to do was have a chat with a corpse. Dead easy.

# Inca Life

## FORGET ME KNOT

The Incas invented many clever and unique ways of doing things. One of the most extraordinary is the *quipu*, a way of keeping records. While most cultures wrote letters or symbols on a surface (like clay, papyrus, leather or paper), the Incas tied knots on pieces of string. The colour and length of each string meant something; so did the type and number of knots. Special state officials, called *quipucamayoqs*, were trained in how to 'write' and decipher the *quipu*, and some people still use *quipu* to record numbers in South America today.

## OVER THE MOON

The sun and moon pop up a lot in Inca culture. For a start, Incas believed their emperor was descended from the sun, and their empress from the moon. They also created calendars by studying the sun, moon and stars — pretty impressive, and handy, too. After all, how else do you set dates for everything from farming to religious festivals?

## POPCORN

Corn was very popular in Central and South America for a long time, but Europeans didn't know about it till they arrived in the continent in the 15th century AD. The Incas cooked a whole bunch of delicious corn dishes, from bread to soups. They also made something called *cancha*. We call it popcorn.

## SHINY THINGS

The Inca empire was rich in silver and gold mines. Nobles liked showing off and wore all sorts of beautiful, intricate stuff made from precious metals. Gold and silver were also important in Inca religion, with gold said to come from the sun god and silver from the moon goddess.

# GETTING THE MESSAGE
## Communications through the ages

### DELIVERED IN PERSON

For a long, long time people couldn't read or write, so the only way to get a message to someone far away was to send a person. This was very slow, and relied on having a trustworthy messenger with a very good memory.

### ON THE WINGS OF A, ER . . . PIGEON

For thousands of years, specially trained pigeons have been used to carry messages. They can fly at over 90km per hour, and can find their way home from over 1,000km away. To think we call them bird brains.

### SETTING THE WORLD ON FIRE

Smoke and fire was another clever way of sending an alert. People placed beacons on hills and mountains as a sort of visual alarm. If a guard spotted an enemy, they lit their giant torch. The person on the next hill saw it and lit theirs, and so on, spreading the warning far and wide.

### JOIN THE DOTS

Things speeded up a lot in the 19th century, with the invention of the telegraph. It couldn't send sounds, like a telephone, only short electrical signals. That required a whole new alphabet, called the Morse Code. Each letter is made up of dashes and dots e.g. A is . _ and B is _...  Sounds dotty, but it was very handy.

### FACE TO FACE

For thousands of years, humans could only communicate face to face. Today, we're doing it again – but via a screen. With video calls from mobile phones, tablets and laptops, we can see and chat to someone anywhere in the world. Sadly, we're so glued to our screens, we forget to chat to people in the same room.

# The World of European Exploration

## *Around the world in a lot more than 80 days*

Imagine setting off to sea with only a slightly dodgy map to guide you. Your map is missing some important bits and bobs, like the Americas and Antarctica. With no telephones or satellites, you can't call for help if you're lost or crash onto the rocks.

It sounds alarming, but that's what explorers from all over Europe started doing in the 15th century. Unsurprisingly, most of them ended up in completely different places from where they intended. They even stumbled upon a couple of continents they didn't know existed. Of those, the Americas were already occupied. Antarctica was free (if you don't count the penguins.)

For the next few hundred years Europeans sailed all over the globe, barging into other people's continents and frequently causing an almighty ruckus as they tried to force their way of life on the people they found there. But they also picked up some new habits in return – and lots of new foods. Up until then, Europeans had never tasted a potato, a tomato, or a cup of tea or coffee.

It was a time of enormous change back home in Europe, too. Scientists and inventors were making all sorts of extraordinary discoveries, while artists and playwrights were creating some of the greatest works of art ever seen.

From the mid-1400s to mid-1800s AD

### THE MAP OF THE WORLD OF EUROPEAN EXPLORATION

Europeans travelled pretty much everywhere around the globe. They conquered lands and established empires in every continent.

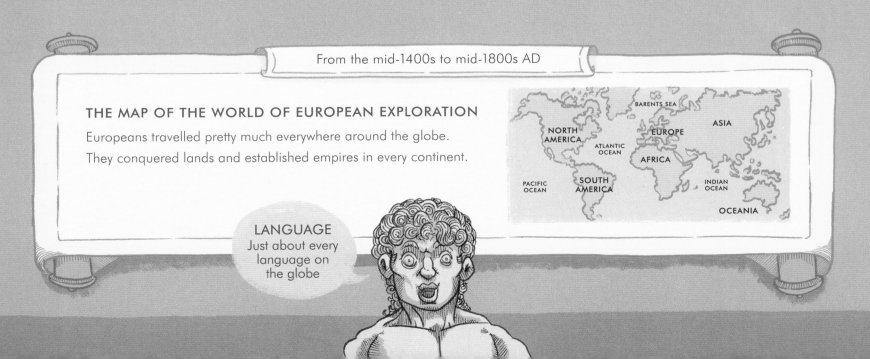

LANGUAGE
Just about every language on the globe

**1 LEONARDO DA VINCI**
Leonardo is most famous for painting the *Mona Lisa*, but he was an all-round genius and a brilliant inventor. He even had an idea for a flying machine. In case it didn't work, he invented an early parachute, too.

**2 SIR ISAAC NEWTON**
A genius scientist who discovered gravity after seeing an apple fall from a tree. He was a bit bonkers, and pressed a knitting needle against his eyeball for hours to see how that made him see light differently. Never, ever do that.

**3 QUEEN VICTORIA**
Legendary queen of the United Kingdom. She loved having an empire and was keen to expand it. By the end of her 64-year reign, it covered so much of the globe, they said that the sun never set on it. Odd, then, that Victoria herself never visited any of it.

**4 QUEEN ELIZABETH I**
Elizabeth had a rocky start (her dad, Henry VIII, had her mum, Anne Boleyn, executed) but she became one of England's most successful monarchs. She promoted exploration, and loved it when privateers, whom she called 'sea dogs', brought her back lots of gold.

**5 JOHN CABOT**
Cabot hoped to find the mythical island of Hy-Brasil out in the Atlantic Ocean. The island was mythical, but North America wasn't, and Cabot landed on the coast of Canada.

**6 METACOM**
Native Americans fought hard against European invaders. Metacom was one of their most famous leaders. Tired of seeing his people treated badly, he led one of the longest wars against the British in North America.

**7 HENRY THE NAVIGATOR**
A Portuguese prince with a love of sailing. He paid for many expeditions down the coast of Africa, hiring map makers, sailors and soldiers – but never got to sail any ships himself.

**8 CHARLES V**
Emperor of Spain, Austria, the Netherlands, Sicily and much more. As if that wasn't enough, when Spanish explorers sailed to the Americas and conquered the Incas and Aztecs, they brought him back loads more loot.

**9 CHRISTOPHER COLUMBUS**
The Spanish king and queen hired Columbus to find a sea route to east Asia. He duly crossed the Atlantic, and landed on a bunch of islands that Europeans didn't know existed. To his surprise, the islands turned out to be a whole continent: America.

**10 AMERIGO VESPUCCI**
An Italian explorer. He proved that the land Columbus had discovered wasn't Asia, but a whole new continent. He was so good at promoting himself that Europeans named America after him (Amerigo) instead of Columbus. Ouch.

**11 ZUMBI OF PALMARES**
African slaves fought hard to free themselves in the lands they were taken to. Zumbi had been a slave but became king of a community of escaped slaves in Brazil. He's still celebrated in Brazil as a hero.

**12 FERDINAND MAGELLAN**
The very first person to *almost* sail round the world. Magellan set out with five ships and 270 men. Many disasters later, just one ship and 18 men returned – not including Magellan, who'd been killed on the way round.

**22 NICOLAUS COPERNICUS**
A mathematician and astronomer who proved that the earth spins round the sun. This was very upsetting for people who believed that the earth was the centre of the universe.

A new (and complete) map of the world of

# European exploration

showing intrepid sailors, dastardly pirates and a very surprised wombat.

**21 GALILEO GALILEI**
An Italian inventor and scientist who's been called 'the father of modern science'. He came up with lots of whizzy discoveries and made his own telescopes through which he spotted mountains on the surface of the moon.

**20 WILLEM BARENTSZ**
While everyone else was sailing through sunny tropical waters, poor Barentsz tried to find a route to the East via the Arctic. He found lots of ice, polar bears and death – but at least he had a sea named after him.

**19 LAKSHMIBAI**
Queen of the state of Jhansi in northern India. Clever, determined and a terrific sword-fighter, she led a great rebellion against the British rulers in India. The British described her as 'the most dangerous of all Indian leaders'.

**18 SPICE**
Europeans loved exotic spices like cinnamon and nutmeg. Their favourite spice was pepper. It had to be brought all the way from Asia and was a LOT more expensive than it is today.

**17 CHING SHIH**
A super-famous pirate. She commanded hundreds of pirate ships in the China Seas, and stole from anyone and everyone who happened to be sailing by. She lived to tell the tale, too, and died quietly in her bed.

**13 PRIVATEERS**
The oceans were full of pirates. Privateers were posh pirates who were actually encouraged by their kings and queens to go and nab stuff from other countries' ships.

**14 SLAVES**
More than ten million people were violently captured in Africa and used as slaves by European nations. Most were taken to the Americas, where their descendants became a huge part of the population.

**15 WILLIAM SHAKESPEARE**
This was a golden age for theatre. Shakespeare packed in the crowds by writing the saddest tragedies and the funniest comedies. He also invented loads of new words, such as 'lonely', 'puppy-dog' and 'uncomfortable' (which many in his audience would have been, as poorer people either had to stand up, or sit on wooden benches.)

**16 SIR FRANCIS DRAKE**
An English admiral and explorer. Queen Elizabeth I sent him off to sail round the world. Drake made himself incredibly rich along the way by attacking Spanish ships. He then helped defeat the Spanish Armada – so probably wasn't that popular in Spain.

# Not-so-great Navigations
## I'M SURE IT'S JUST AROUND THE CORNER

European navigators were used to crossing the (relatively small) Mediterranean Sea, hopping from coast to coast and between islands. However, crossing huge oceans was still a pretty risky business in those days.

No one knew what shape the continents were – or even how many there were. There were no useful maps and no reliable ways of working out where you were. They didn't even know how far away the places they were trying to get to might be. .

With all this confusion, it's no surprise that most early navigations ended up way off course. Here are some of the more misguided paths early explorers took.

**1 CHRISTOPHER COLUMBUS**
Wanted to get to India.
Ended up in San Salvador (modern-day Bahamas).

**2 JOHN CABOT**
Wanted to get to Hy-Brasil (totally mythical island).
Ended up in Newfoundland (totally non-mythical modern-day Canada).

**3 PEDRO ÁLVARES CABRAL**
Wanted to get to India.
Ended up in Porto Seguro (modern-day Brazil. Happily, he did go on to reach India.)

**4 WILLEM BARENTSZ**
Wanted to find a northeast passage to Asia via the Arctic.
Ended up frozen solid in sea ice.

**5 ABEL TASMAN**
Wanted to get to the Southern Continent (another totally mythical place).
Ended up in Australia, New Zealand and Tasmania (an actual, non-mythical southern continent).

# Rhyme and Reason

## UNDERSTANDING HOW THE WORLD WORKS (OR DOESN'T)

Europeans called this time 'The Age of Reason'. They felt they'd taken a big leap forward from the superstitions of the Middle Ages, and were keen to look at everything in more rational and scientific ways.

All over Europe, people's curiosity was sparked by reports of great explorations and the arrival of fascinating new animals, foods and even peoples from far-off lands. Europeans saw their first llamas, guinea pigs and turkeys, and even tasted chocolate for the first time. Science became very popular, and lots of amazing discoveries were made, including the laws of gravity; how light works; a whole bunch of chemical elements and all sorts of whizzy maths.

The arts were having a great time, too. Theatre, architecture, painting and sculpture flourished across the continent. Some of the most famous artists, like Michelangelo and Leonardo da Vinci, were also pretty good scientists (and engineers, and mathematicians...)

# The Transatlantic Slave Trade

## NOTHING TO JOKE ABOUT

A devastating effect of European exploration was the slave trade across the Atlantic. Slavery had existed in all sorts of cultures for thousands of years, but this was the first time people were kidnapped and enslaved on such a huge scale. More than ten million people were captured in Africa and sold in the rest of the world.

They were forced to work in brutal conditions, often harvesting sugar, cotton and tobacco. Many were murdered or died whilst being transported.

They never stopped fighting for freedom, but it was hundreds of years before they finally managed to achieve it.

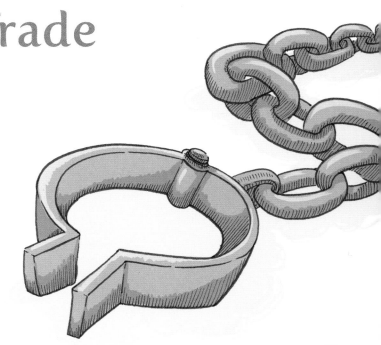

# European Life at Sea

## SHIPSHAPE

If you're going to cross an ocean, you need a good ship. Luckily, ship design was getting better and better, with stronger sails and rigging, and bigger hulls (handy, if you're planning on bringing back lots of gold. Or sugar. Or llamas.) Christopher Columbus' three ships were called *Santa Maria*, *Pinta* and *Niña* (Saint Mary, The Painted One and Little Girl). His favourite, strangely, was *Niña*, which was the smallest.

## STAR-TING POINT

For a long time, the best way to find your way around the world was by using an instrument called an astrolabe. By measuring the position of the stars at certain times, a ship's captain could figure out roughly where he was. It worked *quite* well – but not well enough, given how often European explorers got totally lost.

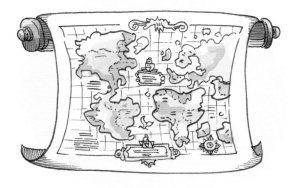

## MAP HAPPY

At last Europeans got tired of bumping into unknown lands and got better at mapping the globe. Surveyors sailed all over the world, measuring the north-south and east-west distances between places (called latitude and longitude). With rough seas, wild beasts and angry local inhabitants to contend with, being a surveyor back then was considerably more exciting than it is today.

## LEMON AID

As if they didn't have enough problems, many sailors at the time suffered from a horrible disease called scurvy. No one knew what caused it – till they finally worked out it was a lack of fruit and veg. From then on, European sailors carried loads of oranges and lemons to eat. They even planted orchards at stopping points along the way, so they could have fresh supplies.

# The Ethiopian World

## *Where we all come from*

So you think the pyramids are old? Well, they are . . . but few places on earth have been inhabited by humans longer than this bit of northeast Africa. People have been living in Ethiopia for a long, long, loooooong time.

This is where anthropologists discovered the fossil of one of our oldest ancestors, who lived over four million years ago – and it looks as if the place has been occupied ever since.

With such a long history, it's no surprise that lots of amazing stuff has happened in Ethiopia. Two thousand years ago, it was the centre of the Kingdom of Aksum, one of the ancient world's greatest empires. A thousand years later, mighty kings built incredible, and very unusual, cities here, chiselling buildings straight out of solid rock.

Ethiopia has always liked to do things its own way. It fought off European countries when they were scrambling to take over Africa. It kept its independence and many of its ancient traditions right up till today. It was even ruled by the same royal family from the 13th century until not so long ago. As if that wasn't unusual enough, the country still uses a totally unique calendar, with thirteen months instead of twelve.

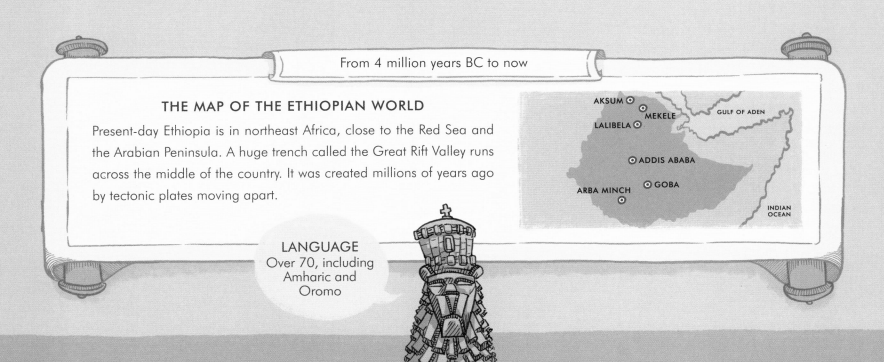

From 4 million years BC to now

### THE MAP OF THE ETHIOPIAN WORLD

Present-day Ethiopia is in northeast Africa, close to the Red Sea and the Arabian Peninsula. A huge trench called the Great Rift Valley runs across the middle of the country. It was created millions of years ago by tectonic plates moving apart.

AKSUM
MEKELE
LALIBELA
GULF OF ADEN
ADDIS ABABA
ARBA MINCH
GOBA
INDIAN OCEAN

**LANGUAGE**
Over 70, including Amharic and Oromo

# A map of the ancient and modern lands of the Ethiopian world

including salty volcanoes, mountain prisons, hidden churches and a very big rift.

**1 WEHNI**

Ethiopian kings imprisoned their brothers (and sometimes their sons) at the top of this mountain, so they wouldn't cause trouble. A lot of these men went on to become kings themselves, which still doesn't seem like much of a consolation.

**2 IYASU THE GREAT**

This emperor was an excellent hunter, a great warrior, and by all accounts a pretty decent chap. He even made the prisons on Mount Wehni nicer for his brothers. (He still didn't set them free, though.)

**3 LALIBELA**

A city named after Emperor Lalibela. He ordered a bunch of churches to be chiselled directly out of the rocky ground – an insanely tough task for the builders. They did an astonishing job, and the churches are still used to this day.

**4 TIMKAT FESTIVAL**

Many Ethiopians believe that the Ark of the Covenant (mentioned in both Jewish and Christian holy texts) has been kept and guarded by local monks for over two thousand years. Timkat is a big religious festival in which people parade replicas of the Ark, called tabots, through towns and villages under beautiful umbrellas.

**5 MENELIK II**

One of Ethiopia's greatest emperors. He loved technology, and did much to modernise the country. He also defeated a bunch of European invaders. Unlike most emperors, Menelik wasn't too flashy, and usually wore a hat instead of a crown.

**6 ADDIS ABABA**

Capital city of present-day Ethiopia. Its name means 'new flower'.

**7 MEAZA ASHENAFI**

A lawyer and judge who is determined to make life fairer for women in Ethiopia. She made such a big difference that she was appointed Ethiopia's Chief Justice. Her most famous court case was even turned into a film.

**8 TIRUNESH DIBABA**

A super-successful long-distance runner. She has won lots of gold medals in major championships, including the Olympics. Running clearly runs in the family: her sister and cousin have won medals at the Olympics, too.

**9 ABEBE BIKILA**

Many of the world's greatest runners come from Ethiopia. Bikila not only won an Olympic gold medal in the marathon, he did it running completely barefoot. Four years later he did it again, but with shoes and socks on.

**10 GEBRE KRISTOS DESTA**

One of Ethiopia's very first modern artists. He caused quite a stir with his colourful, abstract paintings. He even used tin cans, rope and sand in his pictures.

**11 MULATU ASTATKE**

A brilliantly creative musician. He created a brand new type of music by mixing western jazz with Ethiopian folk songs and even church music. He calls it Ethio-Jazz (and probably spent a lot less time naming it than playing it.)

**12 YARED**

A brilliant musician and composer. Yared was inspired to create a new type of music when he heard three little birds singing different tunes. His songs were so good he was made a saint, and they're still played in Ethiopian churches 1,500 years later.

**13 LUCY AND FRIENDS**

Fossils of some of our earliest ancestors have been found in Ethiopia. Ardi is one of the oldest: she lived about 4.4 million years ago. Lucy, an Australopithecus, lived around a million years later. She's named after the Beatles' song, Lucy in the Sky with Diamonds.

**14 ZERESENAY ALEMSEGED**

Alemseged is an anthropologist, who studies human history and behaviour. He's discovered extraordinary fossils of early human species, including the bones of a 3-million-year-old toddler called Selam. That's pretty old for a kid.

**15 AKSUM**

Capital city of the ancient Kingdom of Aksum. It's littered with huge stone monuments called stelae, which marked important people's tombs. The biggest weighed over 500 tonnes and were probably dragged in place by elephants.

**16 QUEEN MAKEDA**

Also called the Queen of Sheba, Makeda features in all sorts of ancient legends. She was incredibly wealthy and is said to have had a child with famous King Solomon of Israel. All kings of Ethiopia claimed to descend from their son.

**17 DALLOL**

The hottest inhabited place on earth. Dallol is over 100 metres below sea level, and has collapsed volcanoes, scorching hot springs and huge pits of boiling salt, sulphuric acid and molten rock. Surprisingly, some very brave people still live around here.

**18 SALT**

For over 2,000 years, people have done the hot, backbreaking job of mining salt in Dallol. There are no roads, so they carry the salt away on the backs of camels. Thirsty work.

**19 ZEWDITU**

Daughter of Menelik II. Zewditu was the first (and last) empress of Ethiopia. As a woman, she wasn't allowed to rule. She just got to wear all the fancy clothes, while her pesky younger cousin ruled for her.

**20 HAILE SELASSIE**

Zewditu's pesky younger cousin, he became emperor when she died. He tried to make the country more modern, but did it in a very bossy way. He was eventually deposed by the army and spent the rest of his life locked up in his own palace.

**21 MICKAËL BETHE-SELASSIÉ**

An amazing sculptor who creates all sorts of fantastic, colourful things out of papier mâché. Just shows what you can do with paper and glue.

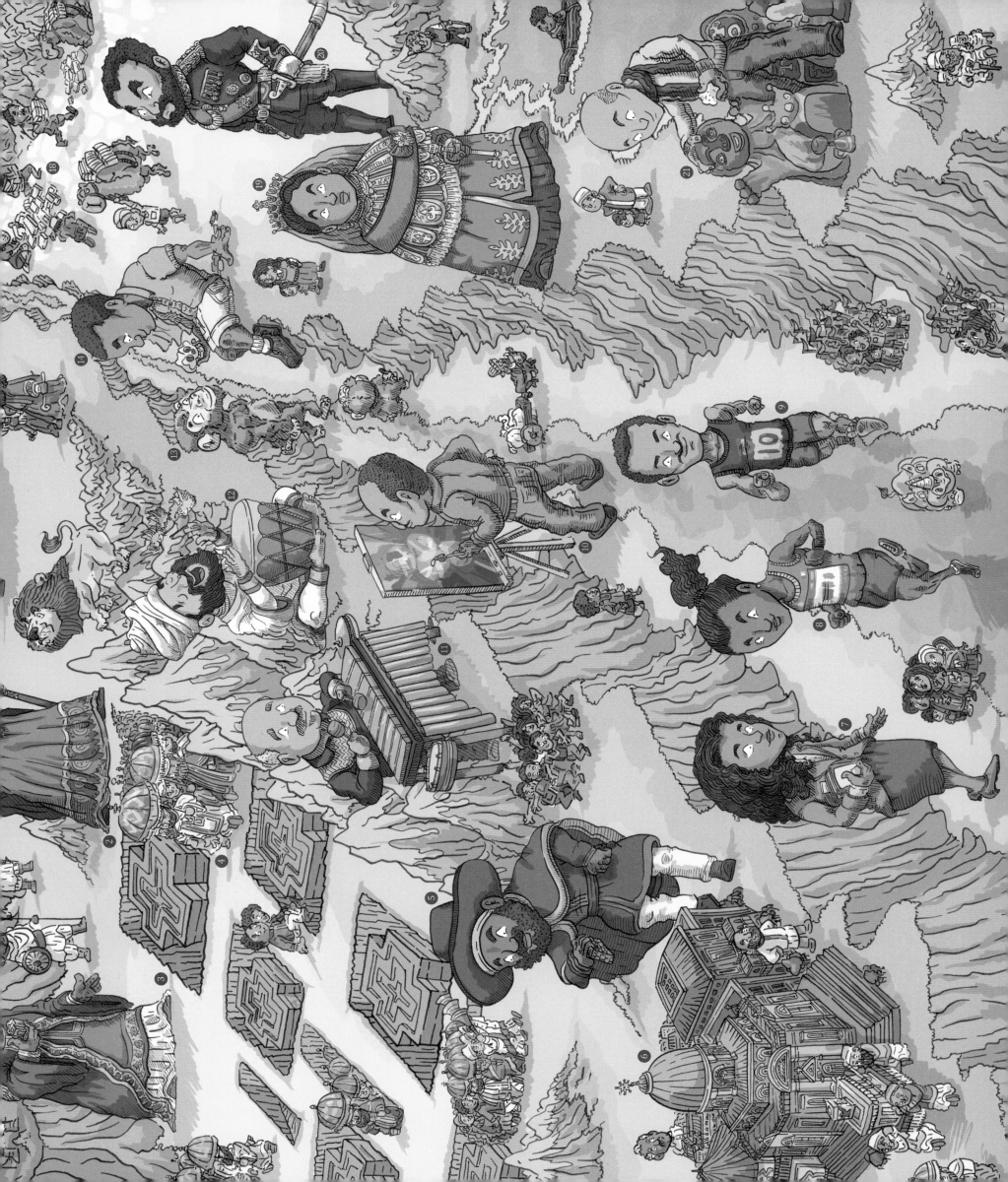

# Full of Beans

## HOW COFFEE WAS DISCOVERED

Coffee is now drunk all around the world, but there's evidence that coffee beans were first cultivated in ancient Ethiopia. Ethiopians have a legend about how they were discovered.

A herdsman called Kaldi noticed that his goats seemed extra-chirpy and full of energy every time they ate some small red cherries from a bush. He collected lots of the little fruit and took them to a monastery.

The monks were suspicious of these strange cherries, and threw them into a fire. Later, they felt bad about having been so rude. They collected the burnt beans and placed them in a jar full of water. Next day, they tasted the water – and discovered that it made them even chirpier than the goats.

People have since found much better ways of making coffee, but beans from Ethiopia are still considered some of the best.

# A Visit from the Queen

## WHEN THE QUEEN OF SHEBA MET KING SOLOMON

The story of how Queen Makeda, ruler of the powerful kingdom of Sheba, met King Solomon of Israel is famous in lots of different cultures.

Solomon was said to be very wise, and Queen Makeda wanted to see if that was true. There were no phones or email at the time, so she hopped on a camel and set off for Israel (with lots of her nobles and servants, and taking gifts of gold and spices). When she arrived, she asked Solomon lots of riddles to test his wisdom. We don't know what the riddles were, but they were undoubtedly pretty tricky.

Solomon quite fancied the queen, and convinced her to stay in his palace for a while. She must have liked him, too, as they eventually decided to have a baby together. Queen Makeda gave birth on her way back to Sheba (having presumably got off her camel first.) The boy, called Menelik, grew up clever like his mum and wise like his dad. He became a great king, and the ancestor of all Ethiopian emperors.

# Ethiopian Life

## A VERY STICKY GAME

*Ganna* is a traditional game played all over Ethiopia at Christmas time. It's a bit like field hockey, with players using long sticks to hit a little ball into a goal. It starts in the afternoon, and all the men and boys in the village join in. There are lots of injuries, not many rules, and the game only ends when it's too dark to see the ball.

## WORTH ITS WEIGHT IN SALT

Salt has always been precious, especially long ago, when it wasn't easy to get hold of. Northern Ethiopia has huge salt lakes, which have been mined for centuries. Salt was so valuable that, right up to the twentieth century, Ethiopians used salt blocks instead of money to buy things. They're not the only ones. Our word 'salary' comes from the Latin word for salt.

## DIFFERENT TIMES

Ethiopians measure time quite differently from the rest of us. Their calendar has thirteen months: twelve months with thirty days each, and a thirteenth month with five days (or six in a leap year). They also count the hours of the day from sunrise, instead of from midnight — which makes a lot more sense, when you think about it.

## GIVING YOU THE (SINGLE) EVIL EYE

Traditionally, the walls of Ethiopian churches were painted all over with scenes from the Bible. But how could you tell the good guys from the bad guys? Easy: Ethiopian artists painted good people face-on, while wicked people were shown in profile. The idea was that it was better to have just one evil eye looking out at you, rather than two.

# DOCTOR, DOCTOR!
## *Medicine through the ages*

## BARKING UP THE RIGHT TREE

Ancient Egyptians and Greeks used the bark of the willow tree as a way to numb pain. It sounds bonkers but, like lots of ancient cures, it wasn't. In the 20th century a painkiller called aspirin started being used all over the world. What's it made of? The same chemical components as willow bark.

## LET A LITTLE AIR IN

For thousands of years, humans practised trepanation: drilling a hole into a person's skull. It sounds daft and, without anaesthetic or disinfectant, it would have been painful and dangerous. We're not sure why they did it, but a surprising number of people survived.

## YOU DON'T NEED ALL THAT BLOOD

People used to believe that diseases lived in the blood, and that you could make a person better by getting the bad blood out. To do this, doctors either cut the patient, or placed blood-sucking leeches on them. Astonishingly, doctors today have started using leeches again in some types of operation.

## I'LL HAVE JUST A WEE DROP

Many ancient peoples thought drinking wee could cure a variety of problems. Wee was no good as medicine, but was very useful for tanning leather, cleaning clothes and even making gunpowder.

## SHAM-POO

The Greek philosopher Heraclitus was very unwell, so he decided to take a bath . . . in a tub filled with steaming animal poo (a common 'cure' at the time). Did he get better? No. Did he die? Yes.

## CHICKEN BUMS

In the 17th century people believed that the plague could be cured by rubbing a live chicken's bottom on their sores. All it led to was a bunch of dead people and unhappy chickens.

# The American World

## *Out with the old, in with the new*

Today, the United States of America is one of the most influential nations on Earth. Billions of people across the world have watched an American cartoon, used an American gadget or sung along to an American song. But it was a very different picture four hundred years ago.

Back then, North America belonged to Native Americans: countless peoples who lived everywhere from the tropical south to the frozen north – until the Europeans arrived. Spain, France, England, Holland and Sweden all scrambled to grab chunks of land. It wasn't a pretty time: millions of Native Americans died, and millions of Africans were shipped across the Atlantic and forced to work as slaves.

But not everyone went over to plunder. Thousands of people settled there simply seeking a better life. A new society took shape, with its own confident identity. Americans boldly declared independence from their European rulers, and made up their own rules instead. In *their* country everyone was equal (well, most of the men. Not women or slaves – yet.) And they didn't want any kings or queens. This new country was a republic, and proud of it.

There'd be a civil war before slavery was finally abolished. But America in the 20th century became the hustling, bustling place we know today, in which everyone believed they could find success.

From 1607 AD to today

### THE MAP OF THE AMERICAN WORLD

The first European colonies were all on the Atlantic coast (Jamestown was the first, in 1607). Gradually, the USA spread westwards, till it reached the Pacific Ocean. Today, its 50 states include Alaska, stuck out north on its own, and the tropical Pacific islands of Hawaii.

SEATTLE
PLYMOUTH
NEW YORK
KANSAS CITY
WASHINGTON
SAN FRANCISCO
JAMESTOWN
LOS ANGELES
ATLANTIC
OCEAN
PACIFIC
OCEAN
NEW ORLEANS
MIAMI

**LANGUAGE**
English, Spanish
(and many more)

# 1 INVENTORS
Among America's many amazing inventors, Thomas Jennings was the first African American to patent an invention, for the method of dry cleaning we still use today. Nikola Tesla and Thomas Edison were pioneers (and arch rivals) in electricity and radio communications.

# 2 MARK TWAIN
Author of much-loved books, *The Adventures of Tom Sawyer* and *Huckleberry Finn*. 'Mark Twain' was actually a pen name – a nautical term he'd learned whilst working on river boats.

# 3 CALIFORNIA GOLD RUSH
When gold was discovered in California, thousands dashed off to seek their fortune. With bandits, beasts and diseases to contend with, very few people actually got rich.

# 4 JESSE JAMES
America's most notorious bandit. Despite his many violent robberies, James became a hero to many people (who probably hadn't been robbed or shot by him.)

# 5 FREDERICK DOUGLASS
Douglass escaped from slavery and became a great leader in the fight for freedom and equal rights for African Americans. An exceptional writer and speaker, he became one of the most famous people of the 19th century.

# 6 THE AMERICAN CIVIL WAR
This terrible war kicked off when several states in the deep South set up their own country because they didn't want to follow new laws, such as abolishing slavery. Over half-a-million died before the northern states finally won. Slavery was abolished, and the USA remained a single country.

# 7 ABRAHAM LINCOLN
President during the Civil War. Famous for the Gettysburg Address, a speech about freedom and democracy. Also famous for his beard, which he grew after a schoolgirl said he'd look more likeable with some hair round his thin face.

# 8 SITTING BULL
A fearless Native American chief. Determined to protect his people's land against European Americans, he led his Sioux warriors to a massive victory in the Battle of Little Bighorn.

# 9 HARRIET TUBMAN
An escaped slave and all-action superwoman. Tubman faced incredible dangers, helping lots of other slaves escape, and worked as a spy during the Civil War.

# 10 BENJAMIN FRANKLIN
A Founding Father who was also a great writer and scientist. Made many incredible discoveries, even flying a kite in a thunderstorm to prove that lightning was electricity.

# 11 PHILLIS WHEATLEY
Sold into slavery as a child, it was quickly obvious that Wheatley was gifted. Having learned to read and write, she became the first African-American poet to be published and celebrated across the world.

## 12 EMILY DICKINSON
A brilliant poet who barely left her house or spoke to anyone. Dickinson wrote some 1,800 highly original poems, and is famous for not liking punctuation much.

## 13 POCAHONTAS
Courageous daughter of a Native American chief. She was captured by Europeans, married a British man and changed her name to Rebecca (which is fine, but a lot less cool than Pocahontas).

## 14 KING GEORGE III
The hapless British king that the Americans revolted *against*. They even pulled down a gilded statue of him in New York. Ouch.

## 15 THE BOSTON TEA PARTY
Americans were fed up with paying taxes to Britain – especially the tax on tea. They rebelled by tipping 342 crates of tea into Boston harbour, while disguised as Native Americans. Nothing horrifies Brits more than a terrible waste of tea.

## 16 THE STATUE OF LIBERTY
A huge statue in New York harbour (its nose alone is nearly 1.4m long.) It was a gift from France to the USA, to celebrate both countries' becoming successful democracies. Must have been tough to wrap.

## 17 LUCRETIA MOTT
A campaigner who helped get women the vote. She started campaigning after being excluded from an anti-slavery convention for . . . you guessed it, being a woman.

## 18 GEORGE WASHINGTON
A military hero who led America to victory against British rule. He then got elected America's first president. Poor guy: all he'd ever wanted to do was stay home and run his farm.

## 19 THE CONSTITUTION
America's Founding Fathers (as leaders of the American Revolution were called) spent ages arguing over the rules that would govern their new country. These rules are called the Constitution. They're still being followed (and argued about) today.

## 20 THOMAS JEFFERSON
A Founding Father and America's third president. A great thinker and writer, Jefferson is famous for writing America's Declaration of Independence. He also wrote over 18,000 letters. Imagine doing that with a quill pen.

## 21 WASHINGTON, D.C.
The grand buildings in America's capital city were inspired by ancient Rome. Politicians today still meet in the Capitol building, and the president still lives (and, hopefully, works) in the White House.

An illustration of the early years of the

# American world

showing brave rebels, clever clogs, angry neighbours and a lot of wasted tea.

# Play it again, Uncle Sam

## MUSIC TO OUR EARS

People came from all over the world to live in America, and they brought their music with them: African songs, Scottish church hymns, Irish jigs, German ballads, Polish polkas and many more.

Over time, different rhythms, melodies and even instruments got mixed up together, and turned into everything from jazz and country to gospel, blues, rock n' roll and hip-hop.

New music meant new instruments, too, such as banjos, electric guitars and drum kits. 'Jug bands' even made music from household items like jugs, spoons and washboards. But some instruments didn't catch on, like the Great Stalacpipe Organ, where you make music by tapping on stalactites inside a huge cave in Virginia. Not the easiest instrument to take to a concert.

# Thanksgiving

## FEAST OR FAMINE

Every November, American families enjoy a huge traditional feast of turkey, sweet potatoes and pumpkin pie (followed by traditional tummy ache.) There are lots of stories about how this feast began. The most popular starts with a ship called the Mayflower, which set sail from England in 1620. On board were 102 men, women and children, hoping to start a new life in America.

They had a terrible first winter in Plymouth (just north of New York), struggling to live and farm in a place that was so different from their old home. Nearly half of them died of hunger and diseases. But the following year, with the help of the native Wampanoag people, they finally had a successful harvest. They were so happy not to have died of hunger that they decided to celebrate with a big feast. The Wampanoag joined them, and they spent three whole days eating together.

There was no turkey at that first feast. Instead they had deer, mussels, lobster, goose and maybe even swan. But the idea caught on, and Thanksgiving became a holiday all over the USA.

# America in the 20th Century

## INVENTING A NEW WORLD

Life in twentieth-century America must have been quite a roller-coaster ride. There were some truly difficult low points, like the Great Depression of the 1930s, which pitched millions into terrible poverty. But it was also a time of great positive change.

Throughout the century, thousands of immigrants arrived from all over the world, bringing energy, ideas and lots of curiosity. African Americans took huge strides forward in their long fight for equality, led by brave and brilliant people like Martin Luther King. And it became a century of amazing creativity, as American inventors dreamed up a vast array of innovations that changed the way we all live.

Some American inventions were small, but handy: where would we be today without the light bulb, the zip, the teabag and even the pop-up toaster? Others were rather more grand. Americans were the first to build really massive skyscrapers, such as the Empire State Building (having first, sensibly, invented the lift.)

The first aeroplane was created by the Wright brothers in 1903. It was little more than a bunch of sticks and fabric stuck together, but it did fly – for a short while. (You needed strong nerves to get in a plane in those days.) And, with Henry Ford's invention of the cheap, mass-produced car, Americans even invented the traffic jam.

Perhaps America's best-loved contribution to the world was mass-produced fun. The first cinemas, radio and TV stations all began in the US, and Hollywood's film stars and Walt Disney's cartoons still entertain people all round the globe.

# American Life

## TAKE THE WEEKEND OFF

Americans have invented many things that make our lives easier, but one of their best ideas was the weekend. People have always had rest days, but it was only in early 1900s America that the idea of *two* rest days took off. One of the first to give his staff the weekend off was Henry Ford, inventor of the mass-produced car. He wasn't just being nice: he wanted to give them more time to drive his cars.

## WHEELIE GOOD IDEA

American Bernard Sadow was tired of lugging heavy suitcases around on holiday, so he invented a suitcase-on-wheels. All the shops thought he was bonkers, but other tired travellers saw the point, and the suitcases became super popular. Lucky Bernard could soon stuff a suitcase with money and roll it all the way to the bank.

## IT'S GETTING HOT IN HERE

Scientist Percy Spencer was testing an instrument called a magnetron when he noticed that the candy bar in his pocket had melted. Instead of getting cross about his chocolate, he tried the magnetron on other foods, to see if its microwaves cooked those, too. They did. His accidental discovery led to a brand-new kitchen gadget: the microwave oven.

## HAPPY ACCIDENT

One cold day, an 11-year-old called Frank Epperson mixed himself a soda-water drink, stirring it with a stick. For some reason he didn't drink it, and left the cup outside all night. In the morning, the drink had frozen around the stick: Frank had accidentally made the world's first ice lolly. When he grew up, he started making lollies for a living.

# The Russian World

## *Fancy emperors, fancier eggs and lots of snow*

Russia has always been a country of extremes. For a start, it's extremely big: over 9,000km across from east to west. It's also extremely cold: much of the land is frozen solid all year round. And, if you'd lived in the days of the Russian empire, it was extremely likely that you'd be extremely poor. For hundreds of years, most Russians were peasants (called serfs) and they lived pretty difficult lives.

Meanwhile, a tiny number of extremely rich people owned practically all the land. They owned all the serfs, too, who were treated like slaves. Right at the top of the tree were the tsars – the Russian emperors, who had absolute power over everyone, and

enjoyed fabulously luxurious lives. As you may imagine, these extremes led to a lot of tension over the years.

Despite this, Russians created all sorts of extraordinary stuff, from one of the world's first cars to great scientific discoveries, music and books. They also made some very fancy (but inedible) eggs.

As time went on, the tsars in their palaces became more and more out of touch with the suffering of their people. It's not surprising that, after a few hundred years, the peasants had had enough – and revolution turned Russian society upside down.

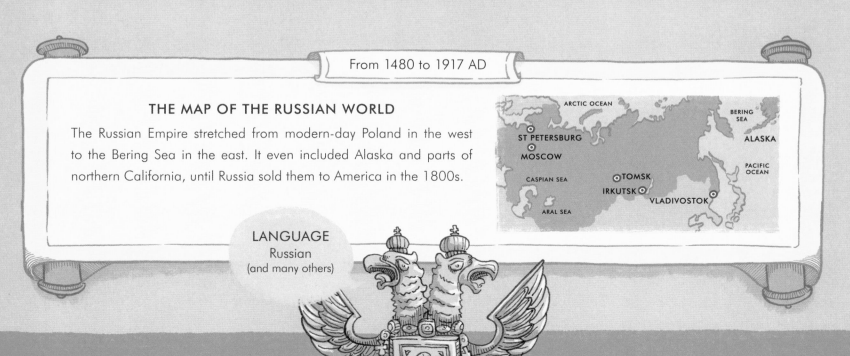

From 1480 to 1917 AD

### THE MAP OF THE RUSSIAN WORLD

The Russian Empire stretched from modern-day Poland in the west to the Bering Sea in the east. It even included Alaska and parts of northern California, until Russia sold them to America in the 1800s.

ARCTIC OCEAN

BERING SEA

ST PETERSBURG

ALASKA

MOSCOW

PACIFIC OCEAN

CASPIAN SEA

TOMSK

IRKUTSK

VLADIVOSTOK

ARAL SEA

LANGUAGE
Russian
(and many others)

## 1 IVAN THE GREAT

There are quite a few 'greats' in Russian history, and Ivan here is the first. The great thing he did was chuck out the Golden Horde (descendants of the Mongols) and unite lots of small countries to form one big country: Russia.

## 2 COSSACKS

Fierce horse riders and warriors who fought in the tsars' armies. Cossacks are also famous for their super-impressive squat dancing.

## 3 PETER THE GREAT

A towering character, literally – nearly seven feet tall, and a bundle of energy. Unusually for a tsar, Peter became a master craftsman in many different trades. He was a great reformer who made huge efforts to bring modern education, science and arts to the country.

## 4 ST PETERSBURG

Peter the Great wanted a dazzling new capital city. He filled it with fabulous palaces and museums – and named it after his own patron saint.

## 5 RUSSIAN BALLET

Ballet is very popular in Russia – baffling for something that mainly involves spinning round on tippy-toes. Anna Pavlova was Russia's most famous dancer. She even had a delicious dessert named after her.

## 6 ANNA AND ELIZABETH

Two empresses famous for their extravagance. Elizabeth had thousands of dresses and made it illegal for anyone else to dress like her. On the plus side, she refused to have anybody executed (even if they were wearing the same dress as hers.)

## 7 VLADIMIR LENIN

A revolutionary leader who dreamed of overthrowing the monarchy. In 1917 Lenin's dream came true. With new government came many new problems, but Lenin is still a hero to many Russians, and his preserved body remains on display in Moscow.

## 8 CATHERINE I

Wife of Peter the Great. She took over when he died, becoming the first ever empress of the Russian Empire. Not bad for someone who'd been born poor, lost her parents to the plague, and spent her early life as a servant.

## 9 ANNA FILOSOFOVA

A brave feminist who spent her whole life fighting to make the lives of women better. She opened Russia's first university for women, and also did much to help the poor.

## 10 MOSCOW

Moscow started as a small timber fort. It grew (a lot) to become one of the most magnificent cities in Eastern Europe. It's still the capital of modern-day Russia.

## 11 TRANS-SIBERIAN RAILWAY

Russia is very large. Getting across it took ages, so the tsar ordered a vast railway across the whole country. It's still one of the world's longest, and takes eight days to travel from Moscow to Vladivostok.

## 12 DMITRI MENDELEEV

A brilliant scientist who created the Periodic Table: a genius way of organising all the chemical elements in the universe. He had the idea in a dream – not the most common scientific method.

## 13 SEMYON DEZHNEV

A brave explorer who was the first to sail across the sea between Russia and Alaska. Sadly, he didn't shout about this. Eighty years later, another explorer, Vitus Bering, travelled the same route – and named it the Bering Strait.

## 14 NICHOLAS II

The last tsar. Nicholas wasn't much good at the job, and eventually had to give up the throne. That wasn't enough for some revolutionaries, and he was murdered alongside his family.

## 15 ALEXANDER II

The tsar who finally gave the serfs their freedom. He tried to make many changes to Russian society. These upset nobles (who wanted things to stay the same) and revolutionaries (who wanted things to change). There's no pleasing some people.

A map of the many aspects of

# the Russian world

including frozen seas, beautiful cities and graceful dancers.

## 16 GRIGORI RASPUTIN

A bizarre mystic who claimed he could cure Nicholas II's sickly son. He bewitched the tsar and tsarina, and even meddled in government. A group of angry nobles eventually killed him, but it wasn't easy: he was poisoned, shot, and finally drowned in a river. (Maybe he *was* magical after all . . .)

## 17 CATHERINE THE GREAT

One of Russia's greatest rulers. She began by deposing her own husband, but then ruled for over 30 years. Clever and cultured, she wrote books, championed the arts and even took the newly invented smallpox vaccine, to show the Russian people that it was safe.

## 18 IVAN THE TERRIBLE

Grandson of Ivan the Great, and the first Russian ruler to call himself *tsar* (from the Roman 'caesar'). He nabbed power from the nobility; blew so much money on wars that the country almost went bankrupt, and threw murderous temper tantrums – hence his 'terrible' nickname.

## 19 LEONTY SHAMSHURENKOV

A peasant with no formal education who invented many wonderful things. Most famous for his 'self-propelling carriage' – a sort of early car.

## 20 FYODOR DOSTOEVSKY AND LEO TOLSTOY

Two magnificent writers (and beard-growers) who are among the greatest authors of all time. Tolstoy is most famous for *War and Peace*, a huge novel featuring hundreds of characters. Pity his poor wife, who copied it all out for him.

## 21 ALEXANDER PETROV

Russia has always produced great chess players. Petrov was so good that he became Russia's best player at just fifteen years old.

## 22 SOFIA KOVALEVSKAYA

A brilliant mathematician who was the first woman in Europe to become a university professor – an extraordinary achievement at a time when most people thought women shouldn't study.

# Serfs you right

## UNFAIR SHARES

How much was a piece of land worth in the Russian Empire? Surprisingly, the value had nothing to do with how big the land was. It had to do with how many serfs lived and worked on it.

Serfs farmed the land, and they belonged to the landowner – who could sell them to someone else if they wanted. Landowners could even decide who their serfs were allowed to marry. It was a crime for serfs to run away (but that didn't stop lots of them trying.)

It didn't take a genius to work out that serfs weren't very happy about this situation. In 1861, the tsar finally abolished serfdom. He reckoned it was better to grant people their freedom, than to wait until they rose up in revolt.

Did life suddenly become better for the ex-serfs? Well, no. Although they were legally free, they were still incredibly poor and were treated badly by the rest of society. And a tiny number of wealthy people still owned most of the land.

Eventually, their resentment boiled over in a huge upheaval called the Russian Revolution. The tsar was deposed (and ultimately shot, along with all of his

family). Monarchy was completely abolished and all the nobles and merchants had their property confiscated. The idea was that property would be shared·out equally among everyone. It sounds like a great idea, but sadly it remained just that: an idea.

The new government was supposed to make life better for everyone, but things remained pretty tough for a lot of Russian people. However, at least they couldn't be bought and sold like sheep any more.

# Russian Life

## VIOLINS AND TIPPY-TOES

Some of the most popular music we listen to today was composed by Russian musicians. One of their most famous composers was Tchaikovsky – and one of *his* most famous compositions is *The Nutcracker*. It's a ballet in which lots of toys take a little girl on a tour of The Land of Sweets. Who wouldn't like that?

## EGG-CELLENT

Tsar Alexander III wanted to give his wife a really special Easter egg, so he commissioned a jeweller named Fabergé to make one out of gold and jewels. These extravagant eggs became an annual tradition in the imperial family. They looked amazing – but chocolate eggs would definitely have tasted better.

## A CLOSE SHAVE

The boyar were powerful Russian nobles who took great pride in their long beards. Bit by bit, the tsars took their power away. Then Tsar Peter the Great took their beards away, to make them look more 'modern' and European. He literally shaved some of them himself at a royal reception, which must have got quite messy.

## STORY TIME

*Byliny* singers were hugely popular. *Byliny* are long poems, loosely based on historical events. They're usually sung to music and, like most epic poems, they tend to go on quite a bit. They're not exactly historically accurate, either. Some characters have supernatural powers – and the Russian hero always wins (funny, that).

# THE WORLD WARS
## of the 20th CENTURY
### *A grim business*

During the first half of the 20th century humanity went collectively bonkers. Not just a little bit crazy, but totally, absolutely, horribly crazy.

War wasn't new, of course. Peoples and countries had been fighting each other for a long time (you just have to look at the rest of this book to see how much fighting there was.) But this was the first time pretty much everyone in the world, from every continent and culture, fought each other.

One huge war is bad enough but, amazingly, it happened twice. Both times the war started in Europe and, because European countries had lots of colonies and allies in other continents, the war spread to those places, too. New technologies like tanks, planes, machine guns, submarines and massive bombs meant that there was huge devastation and terrible violence. Nearly twenty million people died in World War I, and over three times that number in World War II.

When World War II ended, the world was in shock, and many countries had to rebuild themselves from the rubble. Slowly, people tried to find ways to work together, so that they could solve their problems without blowing everything up. Although they could never hope to put an end to all conflict, they at least wanted to have a go at talking things through first in future.

One of the ways they did this was by setting up an organisation called the United Nations. Most countries are now members, and it's a place where they can all talk (and, more importantly, listen) to each other, and try to find solutions to their differences.

# The Global World
## *All together now*

Not so long ago, sending someone a message could take weeks, even if you had a really fast horse or steamship. Now we can send a message right across the world in an instant.

During the 20th century, all four corners of the world (yes, I know it's round, but you know what I mean) became joined up like never before, and life got a whole lot faster. With aeroplanes, we could travel the world in a matter of hours. With rockets, we could fly to the moon. With new inventions like the telephone, radio, television and internet, we could see, hear and speak to each other no matter where we happened to be.

These days, billions of us share the same ideas and experiences at the same time. Whether it's huge sporting events like the Olympics; incredible scientific achievements like the moon landings, or just a particularly funny video of a dog, we're all in it together now.

As the technological revolution races on, where you live is becoming less and less important. You can be friends, play games, work or hang out with someone that lives on the other side of the world. (You can still be friends with the guys on the other side of the street, too.)

From the early 20th century to now

### THE MAP OF THE GLOBAL WORLD

Most places in the world are connected to the internet, and more than half of the world's population can access it. Let's hope they don't all do it at the same time…

LANGUAGE
About 7,000 languages globally

## 1 FRIDA KAHLO
When Frida was a teenager in Mexico, she nearly died in a terrible bus accident. She couldn't move about for ages, and taught herself how to paint. She became celebrated all over the world for her brilliantly colourful paintings (which were mostly of herself).

## 2 HOLLYWOOD
The place where most American films are made. People travel here from all over the world trying to become movie stars. Some even make it.

## 3 JIM HENSON
Creator of fabulous TV show *The Muppets*. Puppet-maker Henson introduced the world to a sensible, friendly frog and a really grumpy pig.

## 4 MUHAMMAD ALI
Possibly the greatest boxer of all time. Ali made witty, rhyming speeches which inspired many hip-hop artists. When he refused to fight in the Vietnam war, Ali was stripped of his prizes and forbidden to box – but years later he won his title back again.

## 5 THE UNITED NATIONS
After World War II everyone was keen to avoid another war, so they set up the UN. People from nearly every country in the world meet here, trying to keep the peace and help the poor. It certainly beats fighting.

## 6 STEVE JOBS
One of the founders of a huge technology company (named after a tasty fruit). Jobs led a team who designed gadgets like smartphones and computers in a way that made them very easy to use. Thanks to him, billions of people now spend half their life staring at screens (and the other half posing for selfies.)

## 7 ASTRONAUTS
The first astronaut to orbit the earth was a dog called **Laika**. The first human was a fearless Russian called **Yuri Gagarin**. A few years later, American **Neil Armstrong** became the first man to walk (well, bounce) on the moon.

## A long-distance view of the Global world

featuring extraordinary scientists, fearless freedom fighters and a very brave dog.

18 **MARIE CURIE**
A genius scientist who made many discoveries in Physics and Chemistry – she's the only person to win Nobel prizes in two different sciences. In World War I, she invented X-ray vehicles to treat soldiers at battlefields, and trained 150 women to drive them.

19 **JACKIE CHAN**
A famous Chinese actor and martial arts whizz. He performed all sorts of crazy and dangerous stunts in his many films (and broke lots of bones in the process).

20 **TIM BERNERS-LEE**
One of the inventors of the World Wide Web (the system that links websites together.) Tim could have made billions from his work, but chose to keep his discoveries free for everyone to enjoy. Attaboy.

21 **CRICK, WATSON, WILKINS & FRANKLIN**
DNA is the long string of genetic code inside your cells that makes you (and every living thing) unique. These four scientists discovered what DNA looks like (a twirly double-helix).

22 **PELÉ**
Considered the world's greatest football player. Pelé won three World Cups with Brazil and scored more than 1,000 goals in his career. He was so famous, Brazil declared him a national treasure. He even became a very popular comic-book character.

23 **THE BEATLES**
A pop group whose many famous songs include All You Need is Love and Yellow Submarine. Their name is a combination of the words 'beat' and 'beetle'. (Luckily they worked a bit harder on their songs.)

15 **WANGARI MAATHAI**
Maathai campaigned to improve African women's lives and to save the environment. She inspired Kenyan women to plant over 50 million trees. That's a lot of forest.

16 **CHINUA ACHEBE**
One of Africa's greatest authors. Achebe realised that Europeans who wrote about Africa didn't understand it at all. His books show what African life and culture are really like, and have sold millions all over the world.

17 **PABLO PICASSO**
A revolutionary artist, Picasso created incredible images that challenged everyone's ideas of the right way to draw. (Either that, or he really thought people had two eyes on the same side of their face.)

8 **ALEXANDER FLEMING**
A Scottish biologist who accidentally discovered penicillin, the world's most important medicine. He spotted mould growing in his messy laboratory, and realised it could be used to cure infections. Lucky he hadn't done the washing up.

9 **ALBERT EINSTEIN & STEPHEN HAWKING**
Two brilliant scientists that figured out how to explain pretty much everything: time, energy, the origins of the universe, black holes, doughnut holes. (Okay, maybe not that last one.)

10 **BURJ KHALIFA**
A skyscraper in Dubai. It's the tallest building in the world (for now. Someone is always trying to make a taller one). It's over 800m tall, and has 160 floors. Imagine if the lifts broke down.

11 **SRIDEVI**
India has a huge film industry, and Sridevi was one of its most famous stars. She made her first film aged just four and was still winning awards and making Bollywood blockbusters fifty years later.

12 **EDMUND HILLARY & TENZING NORGAY**
The first people to climb to the top of Mount Everest, the highest mountain in the world. After battling snowdrifts, accidents and frozen boots, they stayed just fifteen minutes before climbing down again – they had too little oxygen to stay longer.

13 **HAYAO MIYAZAKI**
Japanese creator of brilliant animated films, set in extraordinary worlds and full of amazing characters, including the cuddliest racoon-cat-owl you've ever seen.

14 **NELSON MANDELA**
Mandela's passionate fight for racial equality in South Africa landed him in jail for over 27 years. When he was finally freed, he was elected the country's first black president.

# Jolly Good Sports

## KICKING A GLOBE (AROUND THE GLOBE)

Humans have always loved sport. The Greeks had the Olympic Games; the Tang had huge sporting festivals. Stone Age people probably enjoyed watching hunters racing away from an angry bear.

But none of these compare with the number of people that turn their TVs on to watch the sports events of today. One of the most popular is the football World Cup. Recently, the Men's World Cup was watched by over 3 billion people – almost half the world's population – and the Women's World Cup is catching up fast.

With such a vast audience, it's no wonder players become famous all round the globe. People even name their babies after successful players. (If you live in England you might know lots of little Gareths and Harrys that have been born since 2018.)

# A whole lot of likes

## HOW THE INTERNET CHANGED THE WORLD

The internet is a huge web of computers that are connected to each other. All sorts of information can be transmitted between them – from emails and web pages to games and applications. It became popular at the end of the 20th century, and now it seems we can't live without it.

Some of the things we can do now – like making video calls or instantly translating one language into another – would have seemed like science fiction just a few years ago.

Like a lot of important stuff (water, sewers, electricity), we don't see how our access to the internet works, but a lot of it runs through huge warehouses full of computers, connected through massive underwater cables. Millions of people around the world work on it all the time.

It's not all fun and games (although there are a lot of fun and games.) With the internet, people could suddenly share their own ideas with the whole world. Most of the time that's great, but it can allow some bad stuff to spread. And perhaps we should all take a break when it comes to cat videos.

# People Power

## CREATING A BETTER WORLD, ONE IDEA AT A TIME

It's not easy trying to change the world by yourself, but some people have a go. A lot of the things that make people's lives fairer and better today exist because of the strength and effort of individuals who believed the world could be improved.

All over the world, people are fighting for many different causes, and finding ways of making others listen to their ideas. They show that the world only gets better when people want to make it better (and that there's nothing stopping you, or anyone else, from trying.)

# WHAT DO WE WANT?

**Equality for African Americans!**
1. Martin Luther King

**Equality for the oppressed!**
2. B.R. Ambedkar

**Education for girls!**
3. Malala Yousafzai

**Equality for people with disabilities!**
4. Helen Keller

**Protect the Amazon rainforest!**
5. Raoni Metuktire

**No apartheid in South Africa!**
6. Archbishop Desmond Tutu

**Stop climate change!**
7. Greta Thunberg

**Equal opportunities for everyone!**
8. Woody Guthrie

**Independence for India!**
9. Mahatma Gandhi

**No segregation in the USA!**
10. Rosa Parks

**Equality for gay people!**
11. Frank Kameny

**Votes for women!**
12. Emmeline Pankhurst

# WHEN DO WE WANT IT? NOW!